W.G. Collingwood's Letters from Iceland

R.G. Collingwood Society

Þingvellir, Iceland, 10 August 1897, by W.G. Collingwood

'We went out to see the very places where events so familiar in books occurred in reality . . . For every touch of human interest in the sagas - pastoral, romantic or sublime - there was, and still remains, a landscape setting no less sweet, or strange or stern.'

W.G. Collingwood and Jón Stefánsson

***A Pilgrimage to the Saga-steads of Iceland* (1899)**

W.G. Collingwood's Letters from Iceland

Travels in Iceland 1897

by W.G. Collingwood and Jón Stefánsson

Edited by Mike and Kate Lea

Published by the R.G. Collingwood Society
with the
Collingwood Icelandic Pilgrimage 2012
an event organised by the
Cumberland and Westmorland Antiquarian and Archaeological Society

R.G. Collingwood Society

Published by the R.G. Collingwood Society
Registered Charity No. 1037636
Collingwood and British Idealism Centre
Cardiff School of European Languages, Translation and Politics,
Cardiff University, 65-68 Park Place, Cardiff, CF10 3AS
with the
Collingwood Icelandic Pilgrimage 2012
an event organised by the
Cumberland and Westmorland Antiquarian and Archaeological Society

ISBN 978-0-9546740-1-4

British Library Cataloguing in Publication Data.
A catalogue record for this book is available from the British Library.

The Cumberland and Westmorland Antiquarian and Archaeological Society (CWAAS) published an earlier version of this book
W.G. Collingwood in Iceland
as a Handbook for the Collingwood Icelandic Pilgrimage in 2012.

Letters from Iceland by W.G. Collingwood,
transcribed and introduced by Janet Gnosspelius,
was first published by the R.G. Collingwood Society
in *Collingwood Studies* Volume Three (1996)
edited by David Boucher and Bruce Haddock.

The articles by Ingi Hans Jónsson and Guðmundur K. Steinbach
were first published in
Fólkið, Fjöllin, Fjörðurinn, Part 2 (Grundarfjörður, 2004), translated by Ida Talling,
and are published here with their permission.

Printed by Badger Press, Cumbria.

Front cover: 'Descent of Arnardalsskarð' on 27 June 1897, by W.G. Collingwood
(Abbot Hall, Kendal)

CONTENTS

Preface

William Gershom Collingwood (1854-1932) was a very influential and important figure in the late 19th and early 20th century, both in the Lake District and nationally. He was an artist, author and antiquary, and became a leading authority on the Scandinavian heritage of Northern England. A Victorian polymath, he was Ruskin's secretary and biographer; the editor of the *Transactions* of the Cumberland and Westmorland Antiquarian and Archaeological Society (CWAAS) and later their President. He founded the Lake Artists Society and, after Ruskin's death, became Professor of Fine Arts at Reading University. He translated *The Life and Death of Cormac the Skald* from the Icelandic and illustrated many Old Norse texts for the Viking Society for Northern Research. In 1897, his fascination for the sagas led him, and his Icelandic friend Jón Stefánsson, to undertake a remarkable 'Pilgrimage' to explore the saga sites in Iceland.

They wrote:

'Our one desire was to find the scenes of long ago,—to put a background to the figures of history: and this we have done. . . We have seen the homes of the heroes. They are no longer empty names to us, no longer formless dreams; and with their reality the great dramas of old start into life and action. It is as if a curtain had gone suddenly up: as if our eyes were opened, at last, to the glory of the North.'

They followed a very demanding schedule, travelling for 10 weeks round Iceland on ponies. During this time, Collingwood, a strong family man, wrote a series of unique letters to his father William, his wife Edith (also called Dorrie or Molly), and his four young children, Dorothy (Dora), Barbara, Robin and Ursula. [Dora's children were later immortalised as the 'Swallows' in the children's books by Arthur Ransome].

Abbot Hall

W.G. Collingwood In Iceland

In his letters home, Collingwood describes his adventures and experiences as they take place. They provide a fascinating account of the people and landscape of the Faroe Islands and Iceland in the 19th century and their relationship to the old Icelandic sagas. They make enthralling reading.

During this expedition, and afterwards, Collingwood made over 300 paintings of Icelandic scenery and people, and also took some of the first photographs in Iceland – 'We carried a Kodak'. When he and Jón Stefánsson returned to England they wrote an equally remarkable book ***A Pilgrimage to the Saga-steads of Iceland*** ('*Saga-steads',* see the Bibliography on page 148) which has become a classic.

Many of his original paintings are in Þjóðminjasafn Íslands (National Museum of Iceland) in Reykjavík. In 1988, Haraldur Hannesson published the magnificent book, *Fegurð Íslands og fornir sögustaðir* ('The Beauty of Iceland and the ancient Saga-steads') with 163 of the paintings in Reykjavík, many photographs and an Icelandic translation of Collingwood's *Letters from Iceland*. The original handwritten letters and the manuscript of *Saga-steads* are now in Abbot Hall Art Gallery, Lakeland Arts Trust, Kendal, Cumbria, together with his photographs and

32 of his Icelandic paintings and drawings. The transcription of his letters by his granddaughter Janet Gnosspelius and another 61 drawings and paintings are in the R.G. Collingwood Society archive in Cardiff University. The *Letters from Iceland* were published in English in 1996 (*Collingwood Studies* Vol. Three).

This book is a new edition of W.G. Collingwood's *Letters from Iceland*, with the original introduction by his granddaughter Janet Gnosspelius, plus a second introduction, written specifically for this book, by another granddaughter, Teresa Smith, who asks why Collingwood went to Iceland in 1897. The book is lavishly illustrated with paintings, drawings, photographs, maps and documents from the extensive collections in Kendal and Cardiff, plus one of Collingwood's most significant Icelandic paintings from the British Museum. The paintings complement those in *Fegurð Íslands og fornir sögustaðir* which are in Reykjavík. We also include the original annotated map used by Collingwood which was recently discovered and presented to Þjóðminjasafn Íslands by Teresa Smith.

The *Letters from Iceland* are interspersed with related articles and information as Interludes, and followed by Appendices giving additional information. These include Jón Stefánsson's own account of their travels; articles by Ingi Hans Jónsson and Guðmundur K. Steinbach about recently discovered paintings in Copenhagen; an interview given by Collingwood to the Icelandic newspaper *Ísafold* in 1897 (all translated by Ida Talling); extracts from the family magazine *Nothing Much* by his daughters Dora and Barbara; lists of paintings and sketches; and Collingwood's family tree. Matthew Townend analyses the changes Collingwood made to his novel *Thorstein of the Mere* after his visit to Iceland, and describes the important role he played in the CWAAS.

Many people have been drawn to visit Iceland and the saga-sites both before and after Collingwood, notably, of course, William Morris in 1871 and 1873 and W.H. Auden and Louis MacNeice in 1936. Recent 'pilgrims' have also been inspired by Collingwood. These include the Icelandic photographer, Einar Falur Ingólfsson who explored and contrasted the places Collingwood visited in 1897 with as they are now, described in his splendid book *Sögustaðir - Í fótspor W.G.Collingwoods* ('Saga-steads - In the footsteps of W.G. Collingwood', Crymogæa, Reykjavík, 2010).

In 2012, we organised a modern **Collingwood Icelandic Pilgrimage** for the Cumberland and Westmorland Antiquarian and Archaeological Society (CWAAS) and 33 'pilgrims' saw Collingwood's paintings in the National Museum in Reykjavík and visited many of the places he had painted. An account of this modern 'Pilgrimage' has been written by Graham Avery and published in association with the CWAAS (Avery, 2013). A brief summary is given here on pages 145-147. The Leader was Dr Matthew Townend whose book, *The Vikings and Victorian Lakeland: The Norse Medievalism of W.G. Collingwood and his Contemporaries* (CWAAS Extra Series XXXIV, 2009), had been launched at Brantwood, Ruskin's house near Coniston. Our Guide was Dr Emily Lethbridge who had explored the saga sites herself during a year-long solo research project and adventure in Iceland in 2011: 'The Saga-steads of Iceland: A 21st-Century Pilgrimage'. It was a splendid and most enjoyable week.

This modern Pilgrimage provided us with the perfect opportunity to present this illustrated edition of *W.G. Collingwood's Letters to Iceland* to a wider audience.

Mike and Kate Lea, July 2013

Eden View Farm, Little Musgrave, Kirkby Stephen, Cumbria CA17 4PQ, UK.

Notes for Readers

Icelandic names: The text of the *Letters from Iceland* are printed as they were transcribed by Janet Gnosspelius, with a few minor corrections. In *A Pilgrimage to the Saga-steads of Iceland* (*'Saga-steads'*), W.G. Collingwood omitted the nominative endings for the English reader, and quotations follow this rule.

Paintings: The paintings and drawings are by W.G. Collingwood unless otherwise stated. The titles in quotation marks were written by him or are as given in *Saga-steads*. The number of the corresponding illustration in *Saga-steads* is given in brackets unless it shows the original illustration. The date of the original painting or drawing is given in brackets unless the date is on the painting itself. See Appendix 1, pages 131-136.

Photographs: The Icelandic photographs from 1897 and their captions are by W.G. Collingwood. See Appendix 2, page 137.

Maps: Sections of two maps are shown thoughout the book: (a) the actual map used and annotated by W.G. Collingwood in 1897 (see page 18), and (b) the map from *Saga-steads*, showing the sites of the numbered Illustrations (see pages 16, 134, 135 and 140).

Acknowledgements

The Editors would very much like to thank those who have helped with this project, including the CWAAS and the 33 participants (the 'pilgrims') who visited Iceland on the Collingwood Icelandic Pilgrimage 2012, especially Matthew Townend, Emily Lethbridge, Teresa Smith, George Smith, Graham Avery and Jake Collingwood; Ida Talling for translations; Surekha Datye and Helena Dejak, Nonni Travel, Akureyri; our coach driver Aron Smári Barber; Þorbjörn Hlynur Árnason at Borg; Alyson Bailes, Eliza Read and the English Speaking Union in Reykjavík; Lilja Árnadóttir, Inga Lára Baldvinsdóttir, Margrét Hallmundsdóttir and the Þjóðminjasafn Íslands, Reykjavík; Icelandic Collingwood enthusiasts, Einar Falur Ingólfsson, Rakel Olsen, Ingi Hans Jónsson, Sigurbjörg Kristin Hannesdóttir and Guðmundur K. Steinbach; Þorkell Erlingsson and Margrét Sæmundsdóttir; Dagný Emilsdóttir; Paul and Judi Stevens; Einar Saemundsen; Ingibjörg Styrgerður Haraldsdóttir; Helen Watson, Nick Rogers, James Arnold and the Abbot Hall Art Gallery, Lakeland Arts Trust, Kendal; David Boucher, Sarah Gallimore and the R.G. Collingwood Society.

We thank the following for permission to publish:

Abbot Hall Art Gallery, Lakeland Arts Trust, Kendal for the paintings and drawings by W.G. Collingwood on the front cover and pages 3, 10, 21, 22, 28, 35, 40, 48, 50, 53, 56, 57, 73, 78, 79, 80, 81, 82, 84, 86, 87, 88, 91, 92, 96, 97, 98, 113, 115, 116, 121, 122, 124 and 142; his photographs on pages 7,10, 27, 29, 30, 31, 38, 42, 48, 49, 72, 77, 82, 83, 85, 90, 91, 93, 94, 95, 107, 108, 111, 114, 117, 118, 122, 123, 137 and 142; his diaries, letters and manuscripts on pages 26, 43, 47, 49, 55, 132, 133, 138, 139 and 141; paintings and extracts from *Nothing Much* on pages 15, 32, 33, 69, 95, 110, 112, 118 and 142.

The R.G. Collingwood Society for the transcribed letters and the paintings and drawings by W.G. Collingwood on pages 2, 23, 24, 40, 52, 57, 67, 70, 74, 78, 85, 86, 87, 92, 98 and 120.

Ingi Hans Jónsson and Guðmundur K. Steinbach for the articles in *Fólkið, Fjöllin, Fjörðurinn* and the paintings by W.G. Collingwood on pages 60, 61, 62, 63, 64, and 65 and the photograph on page 59.

Teresa Smith for the painting on page 9, photographs on pages 15, 30, 31, 34, 35, 36, 37, 44, 45, 46, 47, 51, 52, 53, 54, 71, 72, 84, 88, 93, 111, 113, 114, 123, 126 and 127 and maps on pages 18, 41, 68, 89 and 105; Graham Avery for photographs on pages 145 and 146; Þjóðminjasafn Íslands (the National Museum of Iceland) for the paintings on pages 54 and 101; Stofnun Árna Magnússonar, Reykjavík for the image of Gráskinna on page 147; the Trustees of the British Museum for the painting of 'The Parliament of Ancient Iceland' by W.G. Collingwood on page 115; the Viking Society for the obituary on page 130; the Iceland Post Ltd. Philatelic Department for the postage stamp of the SS *Laura* on page 26.

Maps on pages 16, 41, 45, 68, 89, 105, and 140 and drawings on pages 3 and 25 are from *A Pilgrimage to the Saga-steads of Iceland.* The maps on page 27 are from Wikipedia Commons.

Why did W.G. Collingwood go to Iceland in 1897?

by Teresa Smith

This journey started in the Lake District where W.G. Collingwood had lived since 1883; the 1891 census recorded the family in a rented cottage in Gillhead on Lake Windermere belonging to his childhood nurse Harriet, widow of a Windermere fisherman - parents and new baby Ursula in one cottage with servant and nursemaid, and Harriet with the two older children Dora and Robin as boarders next door. In a watercolour by W.G. Collingwood in 1886, shown below, Dorrie (the family's name for their mother) is holding a baby outside the little row of cottages by the road, with a gate and trees[1]. W.G. Collingwood was working for Ruskin (as 'private secretary', or 'Jack-of-all-trades') at Brantwood in Coniston, a journey across Lake Windermere and then on foot of some twenty five miles. A few weeks after the 1891 census, the family moved to Lanehead, a much larger residence on Coniston Water, more conveniently only a few minutes walk along the lake from Ruskin's Brantwood.

W.G. Collingwood trained as an artist, following in his father's footsteps (William Collingwood, friend of Turner). As a classics student in Oxford during the 1870s (he gained a first class classics degree in 1876), W.G. Collingwood was introduced by the painter Alfred Hunt, one of his father's friends, to John Ruskin, then Oxford's Professor of Fine Art (known more informally as 'Professor of Things in General'), and became one of his undergraduate circle, attending

Teresa Smith

1 W.G.C. scribbled on the back: 'Dorrie's Cottage, Aug 1886'. The baby in the picture is his eldest daughter Dora, born on 24 February 1886.

Abbot Hall

W.G. Collingwood in 1886 (self-portrait)

his lectures and classes, joining breakfast parties in his rooms, and taking part in his projects (for example, the Hinksey road-digging project to teach undergraduates the value of hard physical labour). After leaving Oxford he studied under Legros at the Slade, meeting well-known artists such as Burne-Jones whose son he tutored, while nevertheless continuing with his father's encouragement to apply (though unsuccessfully) for academic posts. By the mid-1880s, with his marriage and move north to the Lake District to consolidate his work for Ruskin, he was exhibiting annually at the Royal Academy, and in 1889, shortly after his son Robin's birth, was suggesting to his wife that keeping on a studio in London would pay for itself as well as the rent for the cottage at Gillhead where they then lived.

By the early 1890s, his interests were widening. He was well-known in artistic, antiquarian and archaeological circles in the Lake District; he had joined the CWAAS in 1887, knew many of the key people in the Arts and Crafts movement, and exhibited in local exhibitions as well as nationally. He was recognised nationally as the chief exponent of Ruskin's work, much in demand up and down the country as a lecturer on subjects as diverse as art, mountains, mountain drawing and geology. He was also becoming known for his studies of Scandinavian art and literature and Norse influences in the Lake District. In 1894 he was working on Norse place-names in the Isle of Man and the Lake District (published that year by the CWAAS). He was also drafting and redrafting ideas for his historical novel *Thorstein of the Mere*: *a saga of the Northmen in Lakeland*, dedicated to his son Robin Collingwood, then aged five, published in 1895 with hand-drawn maps, and an elaborate cover and frontispieces with decoration and interlace reminiscent of the carvings on Scandinavian crosses. It was followed in 1896 by *The Bondwoman: a story of the Northmen in Lakeland*, (with frontispiece and initials modelled on the decoration in Morris's *The Story of the Glittering Plain*[2]). So his interest in Norse affairs was deepening, and his contacts with the Scandinavian experts of the time were developing throughout the decade, particularly after joining the Viking Club in 1894, founded in 1892 to promote research on Norse affairs.

Abbot Hall

Lanehead garden

In October 1896 William Morris died. Morris's visits to Iceland in 1871 and

2 W.G. Collingwood refers to *The Story of the Glittering Plain* in *Saga-steads* p.148.

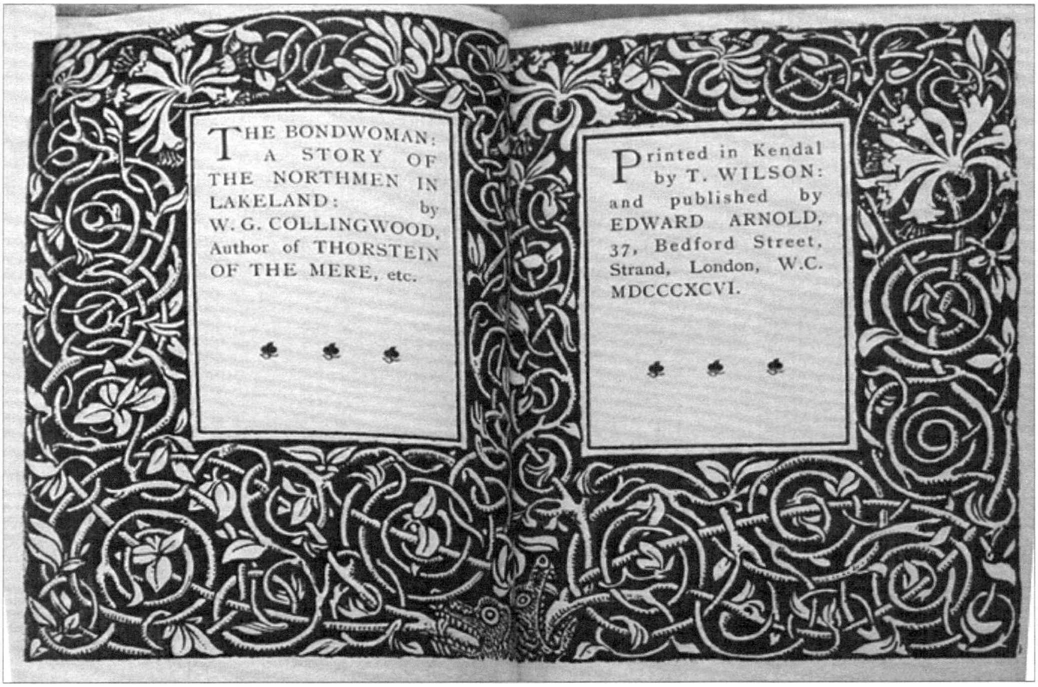

1873, translations and retellings of Icelandic sagas with Eiríkur Magnússon (for example, *The Earthly Paradise* in 1868-70), and his own saga-story *The Story of the Glittering Plain* (1891), had fired Victorian interest in Old Norse and Scandinavian matters. His death prompted W.G. Collingwood's collaboration with the Icelander Jón Stefánsson, who had spent time with him in Coniston a year earlier. In November 1896 they began work together on a translation of the *Kormaks saga* (published eventually in 1902). And over the next few months the idea developed of studying and painting the saga sites on a journey to Iceland – which took place from June to August 1897. During the three months of the trip W.G. Collingwood wrote extensive and copiously illustrated letters home to his family[3], produced hundreds of watercolour paintings and ink sketches, later published, and took a collection of photographs which is now recognised as a unique historical record of Iceland at that time.[4]

What did W.G. Collingwood intend for the Icelandic project? The Preface to the *Saga-steads*, published in 1899, states it clearly and simply: 'This is a picture book to illustrate the sagas of Iceland. It is intended to supply the background of scenery which the ancient dramatic style takes for granted . . . the modern reader, out of Iceland, is left wholly at a loss when he tries to *stage* these dramas, to *visualise* the action and events.' W.G. Collingwood's artistic eye

3 His fifteen letters were transcribed by his granddaughter, Janet Gnosspelius, and published in *Collingwood Studies* Volume Three (1996), and in this volume.

4 See W.G. Collingwood and Jón Stefánsson (1899) *A Pilgrimage to the Saga-steads of Iceland.* Ulverston: W. Holmes; H. Hannesson, A.S. Björnsson, B.T. Björnsson and J.B. Gnosspelius, (1988) *Fegurð Íslands.* Many of W.G. Collingwood's original paintings, sketches and photographs are in the archives of the National Museum of Iceland in Reykjavík; other paintings, sketches and photographs are in Abbot Hall Art Gallery, Kendal and with the R.G. Collingwood Society in Cardiff University.

and 'historical imagination' were a powerful combination, demonstrated in his paintings of the Icelandic 'Thingvellir', as in earlier paintings of the Roman fort at Hardknott in the Lake District made in spring 1889, when he was collaborating on excavations there with Henry Swainson Cowper: one of the resulting pictures, 'The Last of the Romans in Cumberland: Destruction of Hard Knott Camp (end of the 4th century AD)', was exhibited at the Arts, Crafts and Loan Exhibition, Kendal 1891.

The results of the Iceland trip, however, were not very successful. His sketches were worked up into pictures for exhibition; he gave a large number of lectures up and down the country; and in 1899 he and Jón Stefánsson published ***A Pilgrimage to the Saga-steads of Iceland***, with many of his pictures, for which W. Holmes of Ulverston developed new techniques of colour reproduction. Yet none of this effort was as productive as had been hoped and did not lead in new directions for W.G. Collingwood as a painter. Perhaps, as suggested by his son, R.G. Collingwood, the philosopher, historian and archaeologist, in his autobiography,[5] by the mid-1890s W.G. Collingwood's eye was already turning to archaeology: 'I grew up in a gradually thickening archaeological atmosphere: for my father, who as a professional painter was not very successful, turned more and more as he grew older to archaeology, for which he was brilliantly gifted; and at last, during school holidays, I learnt to distinguish the relics of ancient camps and cultivations from eskers and outcrops, was entrusted with the search for prehistoric remains in unexplored districts and the surveying of them when found, and spent two seasons working as his assistant in his now classical excavation of a Romano-British village' (p.80).

W.G. Collingwood did indeed conduct archaeological explorations in Iceland. These included the digging up of Guðrún's grave on Helgafell, in order to test out the accuracy of the oral tradition: 'I wouldn't have done it, but antiquaries have pooh-poohed the tradition', as he reported in his letter to his eldest daughter Dora, written on 17 June 1897. This sounds remarkably like his comment on his later excavation of a burial circle on Banniside Moor above Coniston, published in the CWAAS *Transactions* in 1910: 'it is worth noting that simple inspection and conjecture were valueless in the attempt to explain the site, whereas a few days' digging solved the problem'. Both W.G. Collingwood and his son R.G. Collingwood were part of the new critical approach to evidence through archaeology developed by Haverfield and his colleagues in the Cumberland Excavation Committee in the 1890s. Haverfield, elected Camden Professor of Ancient History in Oxford in 1907 and claimed as the chief figure in Romano-British studies at the time, first saw the work of the CWAAS at Hardknott Castle in 1892, and joined the Cumberland Excavation Committee in 1894, working on Hadrian's Wall for the following ten years to solve problems of its date and construction and regularly publishing the excavation reports in the CWAAS *Transactions* (W.G. Collingwood was editor from 1900). W.G. Collingwood knew him well, and in 1902 was listed in the CWAAS *Transactions* as a participant on one of Haverfield's digs. The 'evidence-based approach' they pioneered (as we might now term it) was later to be developed by R.G. Collingwood as the 'question and answer' approach in his philosophy of history, as he described later in his autobiography (p.124): 'they never dug a trench without knowing exactly what information they were looking for; they knew both that this information was the next thing they needed for the progress of their study, and also that this trench would give it them'. But he learnt it in his youthful archaeological training with his father, sketching and measuring sites, and tramping long miles on field trips.

5 R.G. Collingwood, *An Autobiography* (1939). Oxford: Oxford University Press.

We can perhaps see more clearly what W.G. Collingwood was attempting on the Iceland project if we pay attention to his son. Two things are worth noting. The first is the attempt to explore the historical reality of the oral tradition. R.G. Collingwood continued to draw on his father's work on Scandinavian literature and archaeology throughout his life. In 1936 he joined the Folklore Society and began to lecture on folklore, recalling his childhood readings of the sagas and drawing on folk stories to invent 'a new kind of archaeology'. By this he meant the 'excavation' of the sagas, epics, fairy tales, even Arthurian legends, layer by layer, using all types of evidence available – oral, topological, archaeological, documentary.[6] This, in effect, was what his father had attempted in Iceland, comparing the literary tradition of the sagas with the folk memory of local people and the archaeological remains on the ground.

The second parallel is the notion of 'the historical imagination'. W.G. Collingwood's historical work ran alongside his imaginative reconstructions in his historical pictures and novels. Examples include his work on *Norse place-names in the Lake District* (1894), and his novel *Thorstein* (1895); analysis of records of the 16th and 17th century German miners working in and around Coniston and Keswick (1910 and 1912), and the novel *Dutch Agnes, her Valentine* (1910); as well as his pictures of Hardknott Fort in the Lake District and Þingvellir in Iceland, already discussed. His son was later to be severely critical of what he saw as historical inaccuracy, but for W.G. Collingwood the novels were attempts to portray what people of a particular place and time thought and felt and did, staying as close as possible to the known historical record. In R.G. Collingwood's hands, 'the historical imagination' (the title of his inaugural lecture in Oxford as professor of metaphysics in 1935) became the key tool in historical understanding: the process of 're-enactment', that is, 'getting inside' a person's mind in order to understand the problem to be solved; the example given in the autobiography is Nelson's strategy at Trafalgar, where we have to reconstruct the actors' processes of thought, their calculations and their strategies, in order to make full sense of their actions. As a contemporary historian puts it, this is R.G. Collingwood's 'mode of historical inquiry [which allows] us to turn the surviving relics of the past into history, a body of knowledge and interpretation that retrospectively orders and illuminates the human predicament'.[7] The field to which 'the historical imagination' is applied may be different, but the thought processes look similar, and there is a parallel in a remarkable analytic comment by John Ruskin in his 1872 lectures given in Oxford: '..remember always that the most important part of the history of man is that of his imagination. What he actually does, is always in great part accidental; it is at best a partial fulfilment of his purpose; and what we call history is often... merely a record of the external accidents which befall men... It is therefore a true historian's work diligently to separate the deed from the imagination...'.[8]

Let us return to Iceland. The work done there by W.G. Collingwood and Jón Stefánsson, and by other Norse scholars, could have led in other directions. Their objective as laid out in the introduction to *Saga-steads* – essentially 'setting the scene' or 'giving the context' to the sagas – may only be partially the truth. We should remember Schliemann's testing of the oral tradition of Homer's *Iliad* and *Odyssey* by his excavations at Mycenae, and at Troy, some twenty years earlier. W.G. Collingwood made some attempts to test the Icelandic oral tradition by digging; was there any

6 See D. Boucher, W. James and P. Smallwood (2005). R.G. Collingwood: *The Philosophy of Enchantment: studies in Folktale, Cultural Criticism and Anthropology*. Oxford: Clarendon Press.

7 See N. Ferguson (2011) *Civilisation: the West and the Rest*. London: Allen Lane/ Penguin Books, xx-xxii, xxv.

8 J. Ruskin (1872) *The Eagle's Nest*, in Works, XXII, 269; quoted in Johnston, W M (1967) *The formative years of R.G. Collingwood*. The Hague: Martinus Nijhoff, 25.

hope or expectation this expedition would discover something more substantial, traces of a more organised civilisation, for example?

There is a hint of thinking in this direction. When the *Volsunga saga* was published in 1888, translated by William Morris and Eiríkur Magnússon, H. Halliday Sparling in his introduction compared the ignorance of the 'educated man' of the history of Iceland as narrated in the sagas, to his familiarity with that of Greece and Rome as told through classical literature:

> 'Among battles, "every schoolboy" knows the story of Marathon or Salamis, while it would be hard indeed to find one who did more than recognise the name, if even that, of the great fights of Hafrsfirth or Sticklestead. The language and history of Greece and Rome, their laws and religions, have been always held part of the learning needful to an educated man, but no trouble has been taken to make him familiar with his own people or their tongue... It is, however, becoming ever clearer, and to an increasing number, how supremely important is Icelandic as a word-hoard to the English-speaking peoples, and that in its legend, song and story there is a very mine of noble and pleasant beauty and high manhood...'

As William Morris and Eiríkur Magnússon remind us in their preface: '... this is the Great Story of the North, which should be to all our race what the Tale of Troy was to the Greeks...' How seriously did the educated public take the notion of a 'northern civilisation' to parallel that of Greece and Rome, then or now? There were no spectacular finds of gold and silver from the small diggings by W.G. Collingwood and Jón Stefánsson in Iceland, unlike the Mask of Agamemnon uncovered by Schliemann at Mycenae in 1876. The Icelandic civilisation was perhaps too small; the Mycenaeans stretched across Greece and south to Crete and east to Asia Minor. Yet Morris cast a spell over his era; R.G. Collingwood asked for his *Defence of Guinevere* and *The Earthly Paradise* for his sixth form prize in 1908; and the civilisations he depicted, and the sagas themselves, continue to cast a spell over English writers as far apart as Rosemary Sutcliffe, A. S. Byatt and J. R. R. Tolkien. There is no need for us here to analyse the misappropriation of 'The Great Story of the North' in our era. The challenge for us is to interpret the sagas, their sites, their language and civilisation, in their own terms, as W.G. Collingwood would have had us do.

Teresa Smith

Teresa Smith is the daughter of R.G. Collingwood and granddaughter of W.G. Collingwood. After studying Greats at Oxford (classics and philosophy), and joining digs in Fishbourne, Cirencester, Chios and Motya in Sicily, she taught in Thailand and travelled in India in the 1960s. Returning to Oxford to study social policy and welfare, she worked with the Educational Priority Area Projects 1969-72, the first large-scale government-initiated programme for families with young children in disadvantaged areas. She has continued to research and teach in the fields of community work, family policy and education throughout her working life, and is now a member of the national evaluation team for Children's Centres. She was head of the Oxford University Department of Social Policy and Social Work from 1996 to 2005.

The Collingwood Family at Lanehead, Coniston

W.G. Collingwood

Robin, Barbara, Dora; Ursula above

E.M.D. Collingwood

Teresa Smith

Abbot Hall

'Tea in the Garden' by Dora

'Mother' by Barbara

Abbot Hall

Dora, Barbara, Robin, Ursula with their mother

Teresa Smith

Photographs by Fred Hollyer, 1894

Paintings from *Nothing Much*, 1897

The Route of W.G. Collingwood in 1897

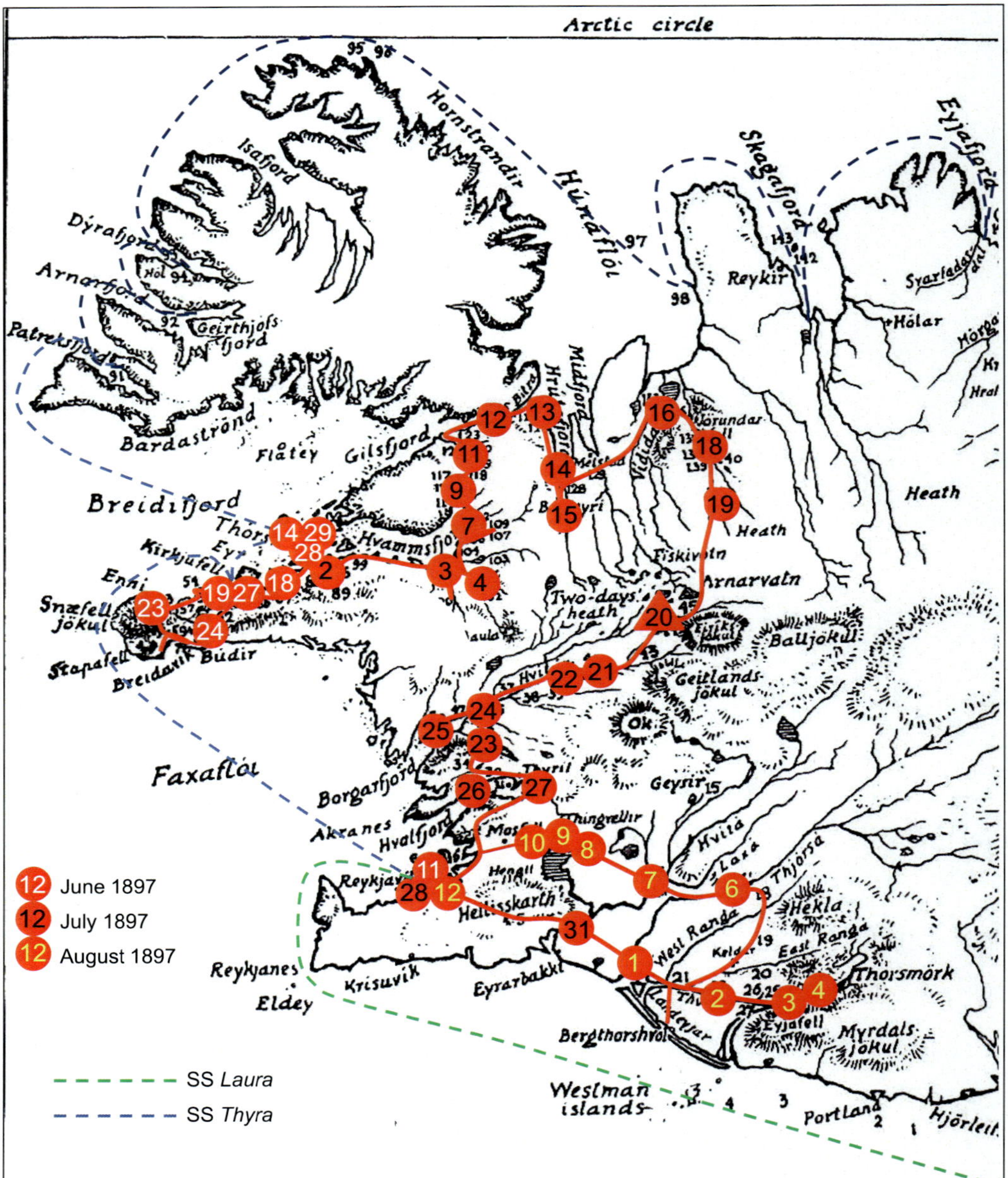

This map shows the sites of the numbered illustrations in *A Pilgrimage to the Saga-steads of Iceland* (small black numerals, also see pages 134, 135 and 140). Sections of this map are shown throughout this book, together with the map Collingwood used in Iceland (see page 18).

The red circles show the the places where they stayed and their dates of arrival in 1897.

W.G. Collingwood's Icelandic Itinerary in 1897

W.G. Collingwood and Jón Stefánsson travelled round Iceland by ship and on ponies. They stayed in hotels, or with local farmers or priests (names in brackets if known).

June

Fri 4	**Depart** Lanehead for SS *Laura*
Sat 5 to Thurs 10	At sea on board SS *Laura*
Fri 11	Reykjavík (Hotel Ísland)
Sat 12	SS *Thyra*
Sun 13	SS *Thyra*
Mon 14	Stykkishólmur (Hotel Stykkishólmur)
Tues 15	Stykkishólmur
Wed 16	Stykkishólmur
Thurs 17	Stykkishólmur
Fri 18	Bjarnarhöfn (Stefán)
Sat 19	Grund (Jón Stefánsson's father)
Sun 20	Grund
Mon 21	Grund
Tues 22	Grund
Wed 23	Ólafsvík (Síra Helgi)
Thurs 24	Búðir (Mr Sæmundsson)
Fri 25	Búðir
Sat 26	Búðir
Sun 27	Grund (Jón Stefánsson's father)
Mon 28	Helga (farmer Jónas)
Tues 29	Stykkishólmur (Hotel Stykkishólmur)
Wed 30	Stykkishólmur

July

Thurs 1	Stykkishólmur
Fri 2	Narfeyri (Jón Stefánsson's relative)
Sat 3	Blönduhlíð
Sun 4	Sauðafell (Björn Bjarnarson)
Mon 5	Sauðafell
Tues 6	Sauðafell
Wed 7	Hjarðarholt (Síra Jón)
Thurs 8	Hjarðarholt
Fri 9	Hvammur (Síra Kjartan)
Sat 10	Hvammur
Sun 11	Hvítardalur (Jón Stefánsson's brother's employer)

July (cont)

Mon 12	Ólafsdalur (Torfi Bjarnason)
Tues 13	Óspakseyri (Guðmundi)
Wed 14	Bær (Sysselman)
Thurs 15	Staðarbakki (clergyman)
Fri 16	Borg (farm)
Sat 17	Borg
Sun 18	Kornsá
Mon 19	'last farm before the mountains' (near Þórhallsstaðir)
Tues 20	Camping near Eiríksjökull
Wed 21	Gilsbakki (clergyman)
Thurs 22	Reykholt
Fri 23	Grund (farm near Skorradalur)
Sat 24	Hvítárvellir (farm)
Sun 25	Borg (Síra Einar)
Mon 26	Grund
Tues 27	Reynivellir (slept in the church)
Wed 28	Reykjavík (Hotel Reykjavík)
Thurs 29	Reykjavík
Fri 30	Reykjavík
Sat 31	Kotströnd (farm)

August

Sun 1	Kálfholt (Síra Ólafur: away)
Mon 2	Oddi (Síra Skúli)
Tues 3	Hlíðarendi (farm)
Wed 4	Barkarstaðir (farmer Tómas)
Thurs 5	Barkarstaðir
Fri 6	Fellsmúli (Síra Einar)
Sat 7	Skálholt
Sun 8	Múli (farm)
Mon 9	Farm near Þingvellir (outhouse)
Tues 10	Þingvellir (probably clergyman)
Wed 11	Þingvellir
Thurs 12	Reykjavík (Hotel Reykjavík)
Fri 13 to Sun 28	At sea on board SS *Thyra*
Sun 29	**Arrive in Leith**

W.G. Collingwood's Map of Iceland

The actual map used by W.G. Collingwood on his travels in Iceland in 1897 is shown below. It is in 32 sections, mounted on canvas. He marked his route in pencil and red ink. Parts of this map are used throughout this book to illustrate his route.

The map was surveyed by Björn Gunnlaugsson, a famous Icelandic mathematician and cartographer (see http://en.wikipedia.org/wiki/Björn_Gunnlaugsson). In 1829, Björn proposed to the Danish government to undertake a land survey of Iceland, and asked for the instruments used by the Danish Navy in their earlier coastal surveys from 1775 to 1818. In 1831, the Literary Society of Iceland helped him obtain the necessary instruments and sponsored him with a yearly grant, as did the Danish government from 1836 to 1846. From 1831 to 1843, Björn spent the summers surveying with one assistant, and in the winters he drew the maps. He started from the earlier coastal surveys, extending the triangulation inland. The hand-drawn maps were sent to Copenhagen to Olaf Nikolas Olsen. The Literary Society of Iceland published the map under Olsen's name, paid for by the Danish treasury, on four sheets at a scale of 1:480,000 using a conical projection. The title page was in Danish and French. Although dated 1844, it was probably not completed until 1848.

Collingwood's annotated map was presented to Þjóðminjasafn Íslands (National Museum of Iceland) on 19 July 2012 by Teresa Smith, during a **Symposium on W.G. Collingwood**.

Teresa Smith

Letters from Iceland*

by W.G. Collingwood

Introduction by Janet Gnosspelius

William Gershom Collingwood was born in Liverpool in 1854[1], the eldest child of the watercolour painter William Collingwood and his Swiss wife, Marie Imhoff. His father took him sketching as soon as he could use a pencil, drawing mountains in nearby North Wales, in the English Lake District, and as he grew older, in Switzerland. For other holidays he would go to stay with his brother and sister at Gillhead on the shore of Windermere where their old nurse Harriet lived with her fisherman husband William Alexander[2]. At Gillhead with Gummers How (Gunnars-haugr) behind them they looked westwards across the lake over Graythwaite (Grettis-thveit) Satterthwaite (Saeta-thveit) and Grizedale (Grísa-dalr) to the peak of Coniston *Old Man* standing up beyond the lake called by romantics Thurston Water (Thorsteins-vatn)[3]. Alexander was a great storyteller with tales of fights with the Scotch, the doings of the monks of Furness Abbey, the giant of Troutbeck, the outlaw of Blake Holm, and ghosts - one just down the road, and a fearsome 'boggle' that met Graythwaite folk coming home late on Saturday nights - and many and many another.

Gershom went up to University College, Oxford, to read for Mods and Greats in 1872, the year after William Morris's first visit to Iceland with Eiríkr Magnússon.[4] He lost no time in joining John Ruskin's drawing school, and soon was quite at home in the life of the University, but in every vacation when he had the chance he spent some time with the Alexanders and was at Gillhead when the news of his first in Greats reached him. After Oxford he went to London to study painting at the Slade School of Art under Alphonse Legros[5] and at his aunt's house in Notting Hill met another art-student, a Miss Isaac. For half a dozen years he lived as a young painter in London until Ruskin offered him a job as assistant, and he spent the next two years at Brantwood, Coniston, working on all sorts of things - local geology - the history of art - astronomy - drawing - painting - and harbour making. In 1882 he spent four months with Ruskin in France, Switzerland and Italy, and from one of their studies wrote his first book, *The Limestone Alps of Savoy*.

In 1883 Gershom married Edith Mary Isaac, henceforth known to everyone as Dorrie. They had toyed with the idea of living in Surrey to be near artists and exhibitions in London, but when a cottage at Gillhead became vacant, Gershom rushed north to see it, took it at once, and the wedding day was fixed.[6] They had a Christmas honeymoon in their new house, spent New Year six miles away with Ruskin at Brantwood, and had a home in the Lake District for the rest of their lives.

Part-time assistant and secretary to Ruskin, Gershom earned his living by painting, his landscapes notable for the drawing of rocks with a geologist's understanding and his portraits painted whenever opportunity offered. Now that he was a proper resident of the Lake District he spent any time he had to spare in the study of local history and archaeology, and joined the Cumberland and Westmorland Antiquarian and Archaeological Society in 1887. There he found new friends, many interested in Roman remains, some studying the carved stone fragments

Some Manx Names in Cumbria

By W.G.Collingwood, M.A., with notes by Mr. EIRÍKR MAGNÚSSON.
Extract from *CW1 xiii*,1894, 403-414.
Read at Douglas, September 24th, 1894.

'It has often been noticed that our dialect does not use "burn" for "stream" as in Scotland and Northumberland. "Burn", from *bœrne*, is an Anglo-Saxon word, not occurring in Norse, in which the nearest form is *brunnr*, "a well", as in the Icelandic proverb, "Late to bar the *burn* when the barn is fallen in," referring to a well with a gate, such as we see near old-fashioned cottages. The Scotch and Northumberland "burns" were so named by Anglians, two or three centuries before the Northmen settled our district. The *old* Norse word was *bekkr*; but this was antiquated in Iceland by the time the sagas were written, and even in the 10th century they used *lœkr* for *bekkr* in local names. This shows, I think, that our district was settled and named, and that a local dialect of pre-Icelandic Norse was formed, by the early part of the 10th century. We keep several words that the Icelanders lost. They had a proverb "*öl heiter með mönnum, en með Asum bjór*" - "ale it hight with men, and with Gods beer"; meaning that "beer" was the ancient poetical word, ordinary folk asked for "ale". A parallel proverb said of barley "*bygg* it is called by men, and *barr* by Gods"; *barr* being the older and less familiar name for the less productive sort, superseded by *bygg*. But as we have seen, both words remain with us, in Bigland and Barton. Tilberthwaite, however, is not from "tilling bear" as some one has suggested, but from *Tjald-borgar-þveit*, "tent-fort-field," seen in Tildesburghthwait (*temp*. Ric I.), like *Tjaldastaðir* (Icel.)'

of Anglian and later Scandinavian origin and others collecting the local place-names of Norse derivation. Gershom first displayed his talent for drawing and interpreting old and worn stone carvings with a description of the 11th century Tympanum at Bridekirk (near Cockermouth) published with characteristic modesty in an article by the Rev. W S. Calverley in 1892.

The growing family moved to Lanehead just a mile from Ruskin at Brantwood in 1891, and to the job of part-time secretary was added editorial work and the responsibility of writing the *Life and Work of John Ruskin* published in May 1893.

In the following August Gershom started plotting Norse place-names on the local map, helped by his childhood familiarity with names and dialect, but with a scholar's care tracing the earliest recorded forms of each name. As he worked up the valley to the lake under his study window the story of Thorstein began to unfold - the Viking's son who explored the river from his father's settlement at Greenodd (Grænn-oddi) and discovered the great unknown water among the fells which still bears his name. Before that story was written down, in September 1894 a meeting of the antiquarian society in the Isle of Man gave him the opportunity for a paper comparing the names of Norse derivation there with those of the Lake District and it was published with notes by Eiríkr Magnússon as 'Some Manx names in Cumbria'.[7] Old Norse inflexions were going through changes at that time and the forms in the Isle of Man were evidence that the first settlers (like Thorstein's father) left the Island and came to the shores of the Lake District when Ragnwald the Dane attacked in 913. Then in October Gershom and Dorrie had permission to excavate old buildings on Peel Island on Thurston Water - a small natural fortress - providing another interlude in Thorstein's adventurous life. On these foundations *Thorstein of the Mere* was written and published in May 1895. 'Thus' Gershom wrote 'sung, or would, or could, or should have sung the local skald' - a man perhaps not unlike old William Alexander, in whom the

Abbot Hall

'Thingeyri in Dýrafjord', *Saga-steads* 94 (17 August 1897)

story telling tradition still lived.

In 1894 Gershom had joined the Viking Club (founded 1892) to meet others with interests in northern research. It was in the week after news of the death of William Morris (1834-1896) reached Lanehead that this new friend Jón Stefánsson (1862-1952) wrote suggesting that Gershom should translate an Icelandic saga.[8] Stefánsson, an Iceland-born philologist living in London, came to stay and between the 16th and 25th of November 1896 they worked together on *The life and death of Cormac the skald*. The source they used came from a fourteenth century copy of a work about 50 years earlier written from the oral tradition, but also from earlier manuscripts which showed signs of tenth century forms of the Old Norse that Cormac the poet (skald) had used in his verses. The 26-page Introduction contains a wealth of information, and also reveals how urgently Gershom felt the need to see the landscape. Visiting the sites of the sagas would be a formidable and expensive undertaking and would take up most of the summer, but Stefánsson must have persuaded him that two men on two horses could do the job. Then Gershom saw a photograph of a jolly little girl[9] with a snowball, and gave way, he would go and make sketches of the sites of the classic sagas.

So in the early summer of 1897 Gershom bought a folding Kodak camera and '5 boxes of films' chosen by his brother-in-law, Sidney Isaac, selected sketchbooks and put his sketching things in order, fitted a plait of Dorrie's hair in place of a watch-chain, drew £50. 0. 0d. from the bank, finished and delivered the portrait he was painting on the Thursday, and on Friday the 4th of June set out with Jón Stefánsson for Edinburgh. They took first class return tickets to Reykjavík at the advertised cost of £8. 0. 0d. and went aboard the *Laura* the same evening. The story of the adventures of the next twelve weeks is told in the letters he wrote to his wife, his four children, and his father.

Abbot Hall

'Drangey from the South', *Saga-steads* 142 (18 August 1897)

* * *

Gershom used his letters home as his journal, but the best record of his travels are the 200 odd sketches he made. From them we can follow the voyage of the *Thyra* leaving Reykjavík early on the 14th of August, rounding Snaefellsjökull and peeping into Grundar-fjord on the way to Stykkisholm; then calling at Patreks-fjord and Geirthjofs-fjord before arriving at Thingeyri in Dyra-fjord, where they were on the 17th. At each of these places *Thyra* anchored to do her business, and sketches were made from the ship, but at Thingeyri Gershom landed and his dated sketch - 94 on the map - shows the steamer anchored off the scattered group of houses of the village, with a small sailing vessel and boats, and the calm fjord winding away into the mountains. They rounded the horn of the north cape at sunrise next morning, coasted along Horn-strandir where the most isolated Icelanders live and saw an iceberg in the great bay of Huna-floi before calling at Skaga-strond and sketching Spakonufell, Spae-quean's fell, where lived the witch who gave Cormac, when he was tempted to console himself with a good match, the advice that turned him into the faithful lover and lifelong poet of a wedded woman who never could be his.

Then they went round into Skaga-fjord to see the island of Drangey [142 on the map] where Grettir the Strong met his death. Next *Thyra* went into Eyja-fjord and, following the dates of the drawings, must have spent one night at least off Akureyri, the modern trading place near the inner end of the fjord where the run ashore on the 21st yielded a sketch - 146 on the map - of the churchyard gate and view south up the fjord providing identifications for many incidents in Viga-Glum's saga. On the 23rd of August they rounded Raudagnup, the north cape, and entered the

R.G. Collingwood Society

'Akureyri in Eyjafjord', *Saga-steads* 146 (21 August 1897)

arctic circle. On the 24th they were in Vopna-fjord, then on past the mouth of Lodmundar-fjord to Sedis-fjord to make the last sketch as night fell, and at midnight anchor was weighed for the Faroes and Leith.

Gershom seems to have been very fit on his return to Lanehead, judging by the whirl of activity recorded in his diary. By Christmas Eve he had finished writing the manuscript of *A Pilgrimage to the Saga-steads of Iceland* and had bound it by sewing up the sheets. It is a marvellous travel book, describing the pilgrimage starting at the place most visitors would take first, Thingvellir, the site of the Althing - parliament of Republican Iceland - already 70 years old when the decision to accept Christianity for the country was taken in AD 1000. Gershom's special geologist's gift to this area were two, first his birds-eye view of his model, and then an idealised cross-section of the lava sheet which, in cooling and cracking, formed the dramatic entrance ravine, the Almanna-gja, and the 'lögberg' - the Rock of Laws - itself, explanations of the landscape printed on facing pages which no amount of sketching or photography will reveal. At the nearby Haukadal Church he drew the 3½ inch medieval ring plate, and then the 600 year old[10] Fairy Chalice and Paten (silver-gilt filigree and enamel) of Breida-bolstad. Thus pilgrim-readers are taken round the south, and Hval-fjord, Hvitar-sida, Borg, Snaefellsnes and so on, with an outline of the saga of the place, and a passing tribute to the memory of William Morris, 'our decorator poet', 28 lines of his verse describing the hero Kjartan's birthplace, Herdholt in Laxardal.

24 The Fairy Chalice
and central enamel of the Paten of Breida-Bolstad

The Pilgrimage to the Saga-steads of Iceland is illustrated with 151 pictures [Eds: 152 with the frontispiece], chiefly black and white reproductions of the sketches, but 13 are 5" x 7" colour plates - a rarity in books of 1899 - and there are many maps and diagrams. There was a problem with finding a publisher for such a lavish book for a limited audience in spite of a tentative list of 'subscribers'. In 1898 Gershom delivered at least 8 lectures, 2 of them in London, and the one to the Viking Club accompanied with an exhibition at Cliffords Inn, but it was not until next year that a publisher emerged. William Holmes (1846-1907) printer, of Ulverston, was ambitious and resourceful and the first copy of the *Saga-steads* arrived on 28 April 1899. By the 1st of October 1901 there were only 90 odd copies unsold, and the publication - by William Holmes - of *Cormac* became a possibility. The translation of this early saga, made in 1896, could now be illustrated with genuine landscapes of no less than 17 of the places named, and Gershom's ambition to produce an Icelandic saga in English was realised.

In April 1905 Gershom was elected President of the Viking Club and served for two years. In May 1906 he was invited to write a book to be called 'Scandinavian England' for the S.P.C.K.'s series on Early Britain. His *Scandinavian Britain* covers the period from the Viking raid on Lindisfarne in 793 through to the battle of Stamford Bridge in 1066 in a brilliant one-volume account written from a consistently Scandinavian point of view and published in 1908. But in spite of all Gershom's enthusiasm, by 1917 in the middle of the war and 20 years after his Iceland visit he was tired of being warehouseman to them, and he gave 52 unsold copies of *Cormac* to the Viking Society.

From the mid 1890s Gershom had been studying carved cross fragments 'of the pre-Norman age' distinguishing those of Anglian design from 740 onwards, from those with Norse or Danish superimposed characteristics dating from after 867, so building up a store of knowledge of the Scandinavian contribution to British art-history leading to his book *Northumbrian Crosses* of 1927. Many items of local history throw light on Norse and Danish life otherwise unrecorded, and the steady trickle of these from 1895 lead to Chapter III 'Angles and Norse' in *Lake District History*, 1925. Gershom died in Coniston on 1 October 1932, commemorated by his son Robin as 'Artist, Author and Antiquary'.

In 1937 just 40 years after the Pilgrimage to the Saga-Steads, a tall young Englishman, Mark Watson (1906-1979) first visited Iceland, he was there again next year and thereafter called himself 'the man who is mad about Iceland'. The war intervened, but in 1958 he located the remaining 145 of Gershom's unsold Iceland watercolours in the custody of Barbara, now Mrs. Gnosspelius, and acquired them. In 1962 he lent them for exhibition in Reykjavík where they were a huge success; and they are now in the possession of the National Museum of Iceland. In 1969 a rationalisation of Collingwood family archive material resulted on 12th October in Teresa Smith handing Janet the packet of 14 of the 'Letters from Iceland' with Barbara's handwriting on the cover, which had been among Robin's papers. From the end of October for four months Janet typed them, one a week, and sent them to Mark Watson, who showed them first to an Icelander living in London, then to friends in Iceland and by February 1971 had picked out the Icelandic scholar, Haraldur Hannesson (1912-1989) to translate them into Icelandic. He then asked Janet to provide an introduction - the first few pages of this introduction. It took until 1988 for Haraldur to complete his translation, select and put in order 162 colour plates of Gershom's pictures (most beautifully printed in Iceland) with a raft of photographs, and with the aid of a generous government grant, publish *Fegurð Íslands* so that Icelanders could share the letters.

And now the really Happy Ending to the story, the publication of Gershom's *Letters from Iceland* in English in Volume III of *Collingwood Studies* just in time for their centenary.

Janet Gnosspelius
Woolton
17 September 1996

'Ringplate of Haukadal church door'
Saga-steads 16

NOTES AND REFERENCES TO THE INTRODUCTION

* The letters were written by hand in various situations and my aim is to present them in print as nearly as possible as they were written. Inconsistencies in punctuation have been retained from originals. [Eds: This Introduction and the transcription of the *Letters from Iceland* were first published in *Collingwood Studies,* Volume Three, pp.1-75, R.G. Collingwood Society (1996)]

---

1 Born 6 August 1854 at 55 Chatham Street, Liverpool (in 1856 this house was re-numbered 87 Chatham Street) from William Collingwood's Journal.

2 William Alexander, one of the commercial fishermen of Windermere (Charlotte Kipling, 'The commercial fisheries of Windermere', *CW2 lxxii*, 1972, 156-204, and C. Kipling, 'The netting sites of Windermere', *CW2 lxxiii*, 1973, 111-119).

3 The Norse forms of place names here quoted are taken from *Thorstein of the Mere* 1st Edn. (1895) 312-316, to illustrate Gershom's understanding of them at this point in his studies.

4 William Morris (1834-1896) made his first visit to Iceland in July and August 1871 with two friends, but also with his translator, Eiríkr Magnússon (1833-1913), the Iceland-born scholar who lived in England from 1862 and was Sub-Librarian of the University of Cambridge 1871-1909. (Morris's second visit was made at the same time of year in 1873.)

5 Alphonse Legros (1837-1911), born at Dijon, France; Slade Professor of Fine Art, University College, London 1875-1892. (The Slade School of Fine Art, a Neo-Classical Grade I listed building, was designed by Hayter Lewis and built in 1872.)

6 Wedding on 7 December 1883 at Kensington Registry Office.

7 W. G. Collingwood, 'Some Manx names in Cumbria' *CW1 xiii*, 1894, 403-14.

8 Dr Jón Stefánsson wrote on 20 October 1896 ... 'Reading your Lakeland Sagas I have the idea that you of all men are best fit to refashion, say *Laxdaela* or *Nicolas*(?). Hall Caine's *The Bondman* and Rider Haggard's *Eric Brighteyes* which are half hearted attempts towards this are favourites with the public.'

9 Sigridur Siemsen (1889-1970) - identified by Haraldur Hannesson and reproduced on p. 70 of *Fegurð Íslands* (1988).

10 Gershom wrote '500 years old' in 1899; in 1996 Janet has added 100 years to that, making '600'.

Boats to Iceland in 1897: W.G. Collingwood's Diary

The entry[1] from W.G. Collingwood's diary below shows the scheduled ships from Leith to Iceland in the summer of 1897.

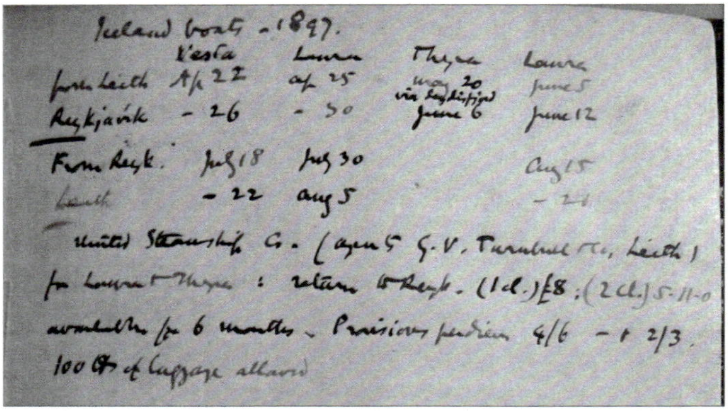

Iceland boats - 1897.

	Vesta	Laura	Thyra	Laura
from Leith	Ap 22	ap 25	may 20 via Seydisfjord	June 5
Reykjavik	- 26	- 30	June 6	June 12
From Reyk.	July 18	July 30		Aug 15
Leith	- 22	aug 5		- 21

United Steamship Co. (agents G.V. Turnbull & Co, Leith)
for Laura & Thyra : return to Reyk. (1 cl.) £8 ; (2 cl.) 5-11-0
available for 6 months – Provisions per diem 4/6 – & 2/3.
100 lbs of luggage allowed

Abbot Hall

W.G. Collingwood and Jón Stefánsson sailed from Leith to Iceland on the SS *Laura* on 4 June 1897. The *Laura* was built in Copenhagen in 1882, specifically for the difficult Copenhagen - Faroe Islands - Iceland route. Calling at Tórshavn could be perilous as there was no harbour and ships had to ride at anchor in the swelling sea while the loading and unloading was handled by 'jagters' (lighters) which were rowed or sailed ashore.

The *Laura* has a special place in maritime history as the first ship bought by Captain Peter Mærsk-Møller in 1886. She was also the first to carry the 7-seven pointed star which is now the logo of the massive A.P. Møller-Mærsk Group. The story goes that Anna, Peter's wife, was ill on one voyage and Peter prayed for her well-being. As he looked up he saw a single star through a chink in the clouds. That star gave him a sense of hope; Anna recovered, and the star became his logo on the funnel of the *Laura*. He wrote to Anna: 'The little star on the funnel is a reminder of the evening I prayed for you so dejectedly and anxiously, asking for the sign that I might see in the grey, overcast sky, a reminder that the Lord hears our prayers'.[2] The *Laura* sailed gallantly until 1910 when she ran aground on the way from Seydisfjördur to Saudárkrókur in Iceland. Many ships since have been called the *Laura Maersk.*

Collingwood also sailed on the SS *Thyra* which was built in 1866 in Hebburn, County Durham. Both ships are shown on Faroese stamps issued in 1983 while the SS *Laura* also features on an Icelandic stamp from 1995.

SS *Laura*

SS *Laura*

SS *Thyra*

1 W.G.C. Diary, end-matter to the 1895-96 volume (Abbot Hall, Kendal).

2 http://maerskstories.maersk.com.

Sailing to Iceland - Leith to Reykjavík
4 to 12 June 1897

LETTERS FROM ICELAND No. 1
To: Robin Collingwood - age 8

Robin at Lanehead

Abbot Hall

S.S. Laura — in the North Atlantic
Whitsunday evening 1897

My dearest Bobbin,

I don't know whether you would or whether you wouldn't like to be here - If you weren't seasick — yes; and I thought of course that I couldn't and wouldn't and shouldn't *bee* — but! ... well - it was a dull foggy morning - four o'clock — yesty. June 5th. that I woke and tumbled out of my berth to see the start. Dr. Stefánsson and I have a cabin to ourselves - sort of lockbed - two drawers in a cupboard - he sleeps top, I underneath - there is a porthole always screwed up - and washing thing and a seat which is filled with our luggage - that's our bedroom. The saloon is just as you expect - with a piano - and on deck is a smoking room - with newspapers. - So I woke up and dressed in a hurry - and got on deck in time to see the pier glide past and various boats loom out of the fog - all booing and belling to warn the others. The water was glassy calm and we went at half speed out of the Forth: creeping and stopping and creeping again. I got on the bows by the look out men and they cried out Bort and Steerbord* [Eds: see endnote], and so on, almost like English. You see this is a Danish boat, and the officers and sailors and most of the passengers are Danes. They are** all rather like inferior English, and their boat is just a clumsily* built English mailboat - no doubt they are nailing good men at the job - the Capt. has been over 100 times so I suppose he knows the way (- I shdn't) thgh. the fog. By about 10 we passed May Id. and gradually turned round to get up the coast. But not a bit of anything did we see of land - nothing but glassy water and fog which was always promising to lift and bits of blue overhead, and one boat after another looming out of the mystery - and gulls and cormorants sitting on the water and never minding the foghorn. We had a lot of meals - coffee early in the morning, bkft at 10, dinner at 3, supper at 9 - and all Danish meals - Let's see - bill of fare none: courses none: table crowded* with plates of cut sausage, smoked salmon, eels in green jelly, sardines, sprats kippered, corned beef, smoked beef - all that kind of thing with white and brown bread and nothing else: only at dinner we began with soup and had a joint and potatoes beside these trimmings. I made people laugh by experimenting on everything and nearly made myself sick. I had also various sorts of drinks: esp. Kommen Akwivit*, a sort of sloe gin that is rather nasty. At the table the Capn. sits at head, then a Dr. Thorodsson who has explored and surveyed interior of Iceland in 16 summers - got gold watch as prize from London Geographical Soc. - very good fellow with the littlest possible nose. Then the doctor of the Faroes - like a Severn who had rather gone to the dogs and brushed his hair straight up - he is a rare good piano player with the best crisp fingertips I can think of - crisp and clinging when need be and lots of contrast in texture of his playing: but he has an evil eye* and helpmeet* - He and a* youngster - hulking boy with a face cut out, you'd think, with the biggest sort of chisel - did a nice concert in the evening: the boy fiddling, and he did it very well - all, of course, music hall and dance rubbish: but pretty to hear in this ripple* and the wriggle* of the screw - and interrupted by the big booings of the siren every few minutes. So we turned in and woke after 8 this morning: I thinking I was all right: and the bit of headache only result of strange meats. It was blowing freshly from NE, and the boat was ploughing away, 10 miles an hour, through white topped waves. I walked up and down for an hour —

Abbot Hall

'Klaksvíg' (Faroes) 8 June 1897

Abbot Hall

'Viking boats'

and got coffee, after a while a gentleman who sits next me came up and said he had been sick - and before very long I felt impelled by growing headache and a sort of something in my bosom to stagger to the taffrail. Well - well - I haven't been bad - and I don't think I made an exhn. of myself. I kept on deck nearly all day - did some sketches even - of Shetlands and Foul* Id. which we sighted 20 or 30 miles away. But I shirked by bkft. and dinner - the steward came and advised me to eat sommsing - and finally* brought me a cup of soup — 'You haffa cope of soup, sir: you wait till* sopper, eat plainty sopper:' I liked the soup, but not the bread, on which lamp or engine oil had been dropped - as sometimes they do at home - nevertheless I ate it, and saw a fine joint of roast mutton going in, with no envy. After they had done the Yankee who is going to buy minerals in* Iceland came and talked: he is very nasal and typical - the French naval officer with legion of honour* ribbon, going out to look after a wrecked hospital ship near Reykjavík, stays in the smoking-room and writes* all day. Stefánsson has been in bed - worse than I. Most of the Danes seem to be all right - but the ladies don't appear - for it has got rougher and rougher. The Laura jumps along and smashes great mountainy* waves into* fountains of spray - when the sun was bright in the aftn.* there were lots of rainbows in them - under a horizon of the darkest indigo blue you can imagine - and dots* of white everywhere - even on the skyline now (1/4 to 9) the sun is getting* down (the time is Danish time, 50 min. before Greenwich) - clouds and showers all about and rainbows reappearing continually in the east - a good deal of splashing on the windward side of the deck - lee scuppers running briskly - rather cold and shivery but nicer out than in. I've got over the sickness, I think, but don't seem to want to smoke, or sit in a stuffy room. I bethought* me of Cocaine* a little while since and found a few perspiring jujubes in a dirty matchbox - of which the little* man in next cabin seemed glad. I'll go down soon and see* if they have damaged him. But its rather jolly sitting here and writing to Bobbin in a sketchbook - on getting up tomorrow we shd be in sight of the Faroes - where we may be able to post - I have the speedwell and forget-me-not still in buttonhole - and the first morning getting out of bed found a paint brush - not mine - on the floor - surely a good omen. Altogether we have made a nice start - and I'd like to have you all with me if I was sure of not seeing you seasick. But tomorrow I expect to be all right and sketching the Faroes - so I may not be able to add to this - dear love* to all and best regards Mr. and Mrs. Willink.[1]

Your W.G.C.*

Monday midday - arrived at Thorshavn, Faroe Isles: come ashore in a viking boat rowed by a viking man - Snow showers - rather sick on the voyage — but halfway there. Just seen the* moon for the first time.

NOTE this letter is written in a small hand with a soft blunt pencil, and words on the folds have been rubbed; it is very difficult to decipher and doubtful words are shown with an * but some are, at present, imaginative reconstructions-rather than 'readings' and shown **.

1 Mr & Mrs Alfred Willink of Burneside, with whom Mrs Collingwood and the children were staying 5 to 19 June.

LETTERS FROM ICELAND No. 2

To: Barbara Collingwood — age 10

S.S. Laura — Klaksvig, Færö.
June 8 1897

Barbara at Lanehead

Abbot Hall

My duckie Bab,

This letter must be to you, being written from a fairy island quite as wonderful as Piwitee. Imagine (you can) a peeled walnut magnified into a range of mountains rather bigger than the Old Man - and set in a blue sea - so that all the crinkles and folds of the walnut are voes or long bays of the sea. In and out of them the steamer goes, winding about in streets as it were of mountains - with never a scrap of flat ground, nothing but basalt crags, grass slopes and sea water. And here and there in the ledges of the great peaked hills, near the shore are green spots, drained with lots of little dykes which are full of marshmarigolds, and rich with the greenest grass - and little brown wooden farmhouses with roofs of turf - and the grass growing green on them - so that the Silly could have fed her cow off it - and gardens with gooseberry and currantbushes - and heaps of primroses - and in the grass everywhere white daisies with never a blush of pink. And all the rest is moor - with ling and grey rocks like the back of Lang Crags, or anywhere above the tree level in our fells. At Thorshavn there were a few trees, small planes,* planted in gardens, and evidently tended as we tend cactuses. But for the rest - never a tree or even a shrub; grass and ling everywhere - and rocks.

But the Piwitean part is the people and their doings.

The men are the real veritable actual gnomes of fairy book. They are dressed* exactly like dwarves; and if they were smaller they would be the creatures who have the house in the story of Snow White. Their houses are toy houses - and their town is a toy town, all little wooden houses - with grass on roofs - apparently pigstyes - up and down toy paths, very steep - all in rock just like Old Man hard and clear, daisies by the sides of the streets - which can't be bicycled or driven in, and - inside the houses, such jolly old quaint comfort - like the house described in Scotts 'Pirate' - sort of cabins - good furniture and brass things and walls panelled and papered with exactly the patterns we should have liked for the Morningroom. The men wear blue breeches with lots of brass buttons at the knee - grey stockings and Iceland shoes with long laces tied round their ankles - sometimes clogs also or rather pattens and long wadmaal coats and jerseys and dwarfs caps all colours*. The women have shawls over their heads and aprons of many colours.

Teresa Smith

'Færoese architecture'

Teresa Smith

'The *Laura* in a fjord'

We got ashore and Dr. Stefansson asked the way to the father of a man he knew. They took us* in* - with the Yankee and the Cockney who went with us, and showed us things - and gave us coffee - solemnly round a round table in a charming room. Then Herr* Niklason* the son in law of old Jacobson, took us round the town. I sketched a lot both last evening and today - and had crowds of natives looking on, - queer houses*, boat* landing places of trap rock in queer little bays with quaint old houses hanging over them - farm in a green patch full of ditches* and marigolds, cliffs and peeps of sea - and this morning a general view of the town - from* a mountain behind - and while we were at that the Laura booed for us and we skooted back, said Goodbye to Fru* Niklason and went aboard on a Viking boat with a dwarf man and boy to row us. When we got to the Faroes it was cold and snow showers were falling, but since the weather has brightened - it has grown sunny and even* hot. We sailed after dinner and passed many and many a fine headland and bay with peaked mountains, and we saw* views on* an isthmus with big mountains all round - great patches of snow in the crags, absolute peace* and loveliness. Dr. J. and I have got up a hill - I am sketching and he writing - we go down and give this letter to a merchant of the place — there's no post office nor hotel — and he will send it on when a ship calls. I hope mother can read this scrawl - but I haven't time to write properly - Tonight we sail for Iceland - but it can't be so <u>dear</u> as the Faroes — I'm in love with them.

The Faroe Doctor's children all came in a sailboat to meet the ship and crowded up on to it - he is the man like Mr. Severn[1] - a good chap - and it was pretty to see the children meet their daddy.

Best love to you all — from the <u>Fairy</u> Islands and your W. G. C.

NOTE: Barbara Collingwood, W.G. Collingwood's second daughter, was the family authority on fairies, and with her elder sister Dora had invented and chronicled events in the imaginary country of *Piwitee*, an island with an ideal climate, peopled largely by princesses and fairies. Robin, on behalf of himself and his younger sister Ursula, had replied by inventing a country called *Jipandland* whose naval forces were pretty formidable.

Words with an * are doubtful readings.

Abbot Hall

'Thingnes'

1 Arthur Severn R.I., J.P., (1842-1931) who married Joan Ruskin Agnew, Ruskin's cousin, in 1871, and when in Coniston lived at Brantwood.

Nothing Much - The Fairy Islands

Nothing Much was a Collingwood family journal, edited by Collingwood's eldest daughter Dora, which ran from 1896 to 1903, with a final, brief re-invention in 1905 as *What Ho! A Summer Annual.*[1] The July 1897 issue of *Nothing Much* commemorated the Diamond Jubilee of Queen Victoria, which was celebrated on Sunday 20 June, and gave some 'News from Iceland' and a painting of 'The Fairy Islands' by Barbara Collingwood. W.G. Collingwood was in Grundarfjörður for the Jubilee and not feeling well, though he painted and drew Grundarfoss on the following Tuesday.

1 M. Townend, (2009) *The Vikings and Victorian Lakeland: The Norse Medievalism of W.G. Collingwood and his Contemporaries*, CWAAS Extra Series, XXXIV, p.83.

Abbot Hall

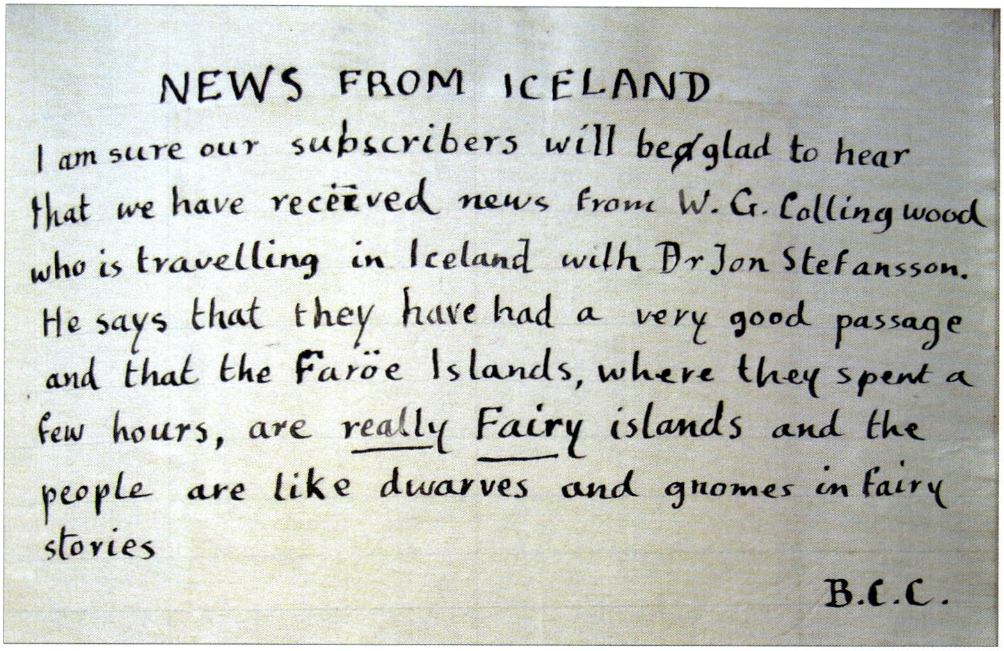

NEWS FROM ICELAND

I am sure our subscribers will be glad to hear that we have received news from W. G. Collingwood who is travelling in Iceland with Dr Jon Stefansson. He says that they have had a very good passage and that the Faröe Islands, where they spent a few hours, are <u>really</u> <u>Fairy</u> islands and the people are like dwarves and gnomes in fairy stories

B.C.C.

Abbot Hall

Abbot Hall

LETTERS FROM ICELAND No. 3

To: Mrs. Collingwood

Hotel Island, Reykjavík
June 11, 1897

My darling Molly,

This will be headquarters - and postal address - and to this address please send two 1/2 pans or tubes of cobalt and one of pink madder - say three of cobalt and 2 of pink madder - when you can get them. There isn't such a thing as a pan of moist colours, still less a tube, in the whole country.

Well - the begging being done - I'll continue the tale of our travels. I wrote to Rob from Thorshaven and to Bab from Klaksvig in the Fairy Islands and now I'm in Niceland. We arrived this morning early after a splendid passage - just a week's journey. I was rather sick on Whitsunday - picked up on Whitmonday; - but caught a cold somehow, which nevertheless has not prevented my being very well and enjoying myself, and making lots of sketches. At Klaksvig in the Faroes, we went to the post - which was also the Governor's - who is postman — and he came out as we debated about dropping the letter in the box; asked us in; gave us cigars and took us aboard our ship - which soon after sailed through wild cliffs, threading its way out, at midnight, from the fjord, in the most romantic scenery you can imagine - I sketched hard till past midnight - and even painted one sketch just at twelve - though it was a rough sea and a cloudy sky. When we saw no more and it was broad daylight again after a short interval of twilight we turned in - not a bit sick, and spent the next day - of splendid sunshine - in working up Faroe sketches, sitting in the deckhouse, and as well and comfortable as in the Morning Room at Lanehead. The French legion of honour officer entertained us at meals with stories in perfect French-English of ballooning with Flammarion, fighting in 1870, and how he got a bath in the bathroom aboard the Laura. I'll try to do him when I get home - but it's too long to write now. One of the passengers, a merchant of West Iceland, gave us a lot of advice about places and travelling - and Dr. Thorodsson was very nice and interesting about his explorations in the interior - so the day passed - and next day early in the morning we sighted Iceland. I sketched the glaciers and coast - and in the afternoon we came to the Westmann Islands - still more wonderful crags than the Faroes, but not so cuddly - there* lone cliffs with innumerable gulls, and a few huts. There we anchored for a while and took on board the M.P. for the islands, an antiquary who lives in Copenhagen, and had been seeing his constituents on the way to Althing. The boat took off two cargoes of corrugated iron and other goods and all the while the sun shone on the blue sea, and huge spouts of spray leaped up from skerries, and the wind whirled drifts of foam up the crags.

Teresa Smith

'Vestmannaeyjar'

'Eyjafjallajökull' (*Saga-steads* 3) (10 June 1897)

I got two fair sketches in colour, and at dinnertime - about four o'clock we were off again - The fiddles (don't they call them?) on the table and all the dishes and forks rolling about. It quieted a little when we got before the wind, but the loss of so much cargo made the Laura roll tremendously in the big waves of the Atlantic. Near midnight we again sighted the Iceland coast - and I sketched the sunset above it - a hazy sky of opalescent colour which everybody was anxious to tell me was not a fine sunset for Iceland; - and finally turning in, woke in Reykjavík harbour.

It is a brilliant morning — and a strong east wind made even the little waves of the open roadstead white and blue - Such a blue sky, hard and clear: and halfway round the panorama snow topped mountains. The straggling town of wooden and iron houses runs along a green promontory - poor and mean looking enough and without any picturesque character, but the distance tells one that.

'Boat taking in roofing iron'

10. p.m. - Here Dr. Stefansson came and took me out to see the sunset - yellow round disc going down over the green bay & mountains pink and purple around it - a thing I couldn't set to work painting now, but enough to make a grand picture for

Teresa Smith

'The pier'

Mr. Severn - as indeed all the coast scenery I have seen - I feel that he would do fine things at the Faroes and indeed everywhere along the line we have come - and the sea alone is subject enough in its varying colours and shapes.

Well, we came ashore in a jumpy little boat - shipping one wave that would have soaked me but for my mackintosh; and landed at a slip like the old Birkenhead ferry; near which was the wrecked French hospital ship which the Frenchman had come to inspect for repairs. Lots of rough craft big and little - and quantities of boxes and bales* and timber and roofing iron lay about in dirty confusion. The town is all wood and iron - I asked why, and they said it was because of earthquakes, which make stone houses dangerous; though they have stone for ever lying about; but no lime for mortar, and apparently they don't know how to do dry walling, and there are only 2 or 3 masons in the place. The hotel is rough - with walls inside boarded and painted ugly colours. The women wear the black cap with long tassel in a silver tube, and plaits of hair. The men have Iceland shoes, but no particular costume. Everybody looks poor and the place entirely forlorn and heartbroken with bleakness and neglect and apparent repression (so it seemed to me) on the part of Those who might encourage life and comfort and the things that make people prosper. There is dirt and disorder and unfinishedness everywhere; and the whole town is only as big as Bowness, but a hundredfold uglier and untidier.

However - to set off against this, I have seen many fine people to whom Stefansson took me: The head of the college Dr. Olsen - I don't know how many s's he has - the finance minister, a very nice old man, grandfather of the little snowballing girl in the photograph, that made me say I would go to Iceland - do you remember? - I told him so, and he seemed quite puzzled - when I spied the same photograph in the drawing room, and said <u>that</u> was what made me come. Then there was Dr. Finnur Jónsson from Copenhagen - a distinguished antiquary - who is going to explore saga-sites like us - only taking his wife and boy, at which everybody is scandalized - and a fat German, Dr. Kahle, going likewise to look up antiquities. Also the editor of the paper, a tall and sturdy young man whom Magnússon has got into a row with a libel on the Governor published lately - he will probably go to prison and seems to think it a lark. We saw also a shopkeeper in a poor little shop - a radical friend of Magnússon's - who wanted me to take something, and I chose a toffee drop. They all give one things, and Stefansson tells them our plans and cracks me up (in Icelandic) before my blushing face

Teresa Smith

'Thorvaldsson's monument and French Consulate'

- We went to the printing office - and the library and saw ancient MSS and printed books - and the Natural History Museum with the curator, a poor old chap who paints fish and pollywogs very well in the archaic style - and gets £2.12.0. a year as curator of the collection in an attic up a ladder. We saw also the keeper of the big 'Edinburgh' store; he is a relation of Stefansson's and married to an Englishwoman: - various teachers at the schools; the governor's secretary, a swagger young man in a tin box house with odds and ends of furniture of the costly kind stood about - but very polite - and I hardly remember how many more - of high and low. They all seemed interested in this* enterprise of painting saga sites, and I expect I shall have to give an exhibition of the sketches before I get away. Only the 20 sketches have used up one pan of cobalt, and I could find only shilling boxes of child's paints in the best shops. Hence the prayer for colours. I have paper enough.

Teresa Smith

'Cathedral front and monument to Jonas Hallgrímsson'

Tomorrow we go aboard the 'Thyra' at night and start for the North - to get the midnight sun behind Gretti's island Drangey - you can find Sturlunga saga Vol II in top shelf, left hand side, of bookcase to left of study door - and map in pocket at end of book; and so follow the route. Thence we zigzag back through the west, and get here in a month or so - which will be the time I must pass before hearing from you: but I hope and trust you are all well and happy: and I think much of you all. It is 20 minutes to eleven and I still write by the window.

I don't know yet how long we shall need. It will depend so much on the rate at which the work gets done - the weather may delay us sometimes: and after getting back in a month we have the south part to do which will not take so long. But I am getting my hand in, and

Teresa Smith

'College Library'

Teresa Smith

'Suburban villas of Reykjavík'

I like what I have done.

The clothes I have do very well, so I don't expect to have to buy more. We have bought some books, and I have asked to be elected to the Iceland antiquarian society and to have their back numbers of proceedings - so bang goes ten and saxpence. But our tickets will take us the rest of the voyage - and we shall spend little in the land travelling, and have return tickets ready.

I have taken three dozen snapshots too.

(This is the end) Our Yankee is going on with us - and a couple of merchants, and a lady something like Mrs. A W Simpson[1] - so we know our fellow voyagers along the fjords. Skagafjordur is where we land. I'll write whenever I can - even if the letters can't go at once. All these three will probably reach you together.

With dearest love,
Your W. G. Collingwood.

1 Wife of the Quaker woodcarver of Kendal.

LETTERS FROM ICELAND No. 4

To: his father, William Collingwood, at Bristol.

Hotel Island, Reykjavík, Iceland.
June 11, 1897

My dear Father,

We arrived here this morning after a fine voyage - just a week after leaving home. At starting from Leith it was foggy and calm - and so all the first day. But on Whitsunday I was rather seasick and very cold - and we saw nothing but outlying crags of Shetland. The next day we came, in cold snow showers to the Faroes - wild basaltic mountains sticking up out of the Atlantic - and anchored in Thórshavn bay - went ashore and foregathered with kindly people in the most picturesque houses imaginable - rather like Swiss[1] in manners and way of living: the men in blue breeches and grey stockings - stocking caps and queer* brown coats of wadmaal. I sketched a good deal in the middle of jabbering crowds - who talk a language of their own that sounds just like English, but isn't. - We sailed in and out of wild lochs among crags and mountains to another village which is an ideal retreat - like Switzerland submerged to 2000 feet or higher - no trees but rocks and snow on their tops - and chalets and the greenest fields. Thence we came - passing the last gates of the sea-mountains at midnight, and I sketching all the while - to open sea again. I was seasick no more, and enjoyed the roll of the sea, and the wind, and sun, mightily. After another day out of sight of land we saw the alps and glaciers - pink and purple and cream above the tossing blue and white. I snatched a few impressions of the coast

Abbot Hall

'Boat bringing Dr. Valter Gudmundsson aboard the *Laura*'

line - in colour - and then we were at the Westmann Islands - still ruggeder and savager than the Faroes - in blazing sun and violent gusts of wind, while the M.P. for the islands came aboard in a big rough sea-boat manned by a crowd of rough oilskin-trousered constituents. He is an antiquary and a swell, on his way to Althing which soon opens here. There were several good men on board; one, the scientific explorer of Iceland, bound on his 16th or 17th trip to survey glaciers; - another a Danish ordnance surveyor at work on the Faroes: another a French officer, legion of honour, sent out to recover a wrecked French ship in the harbour here. Also a Yankee going to get minerals - and a Cockney going to put Cadbury's Cocoa on the Icelandic market: and so forth. Since I have been here, Dr Stefánsson has taken me round to most of the interesting and important people - who all take much interest in our expedition - for they all think a deal of their sagas, and want them to be known in England.

Reykjavík is a poor place - neglected and bleak - a mere village of wood and iron houses: - but there are many good and fine people living here, in what we should call poverty and dulness. The only 'artist' is a poor old man who has made a museum of birds, and eggs, and fishes - and drawn them with penny paints which he complains won't keep moist after four years: and his landscapes are of the very primitive type. He took us over his museum and gave me his books. Everybody was most kind and nice to us - of course, to Stefánsson who knows everybody.

I have done a lot of sketches already, about 20, and used up a pan of cobalt - to my horror, as I find there are no paints to be had in Iceland: but I have written to Dorrie[2] to send me some more. Now that I am getting my hand in I expect a big harvest. We hope to start tomorrow by a steamer to the north - right into the Arctic Circle so that we shall paint the midnight sun behind the romantic island of Grettir the outlaw to begin with - and work back over land, visiting all the scenes of the sagas and trying to make small pictures of them. I am working with a small book, of which the double page gives an Octavo imperial sketch, for better carriage on this scrambling tour, where every ounce of luggage has to be considered. After getting back here in a month - and perhaps finding letters to this address - we hope to take a second shorter tour with a bigger drawing board to the most important places. We are very well and find everything going nicely.

If you have a mind to write address here shortly after getting this. I will write when there is opportunity: but you may believe that we are all right. It seems we shall be well received everywhere - and helped on our way by everyone.

Best love to you both. Your W. G. C.

P.S. It is a quarter to twelve midnight & I am still writing by the window, and not 'trying my eyes', after a splendid sunset over the bay and the Alpine mountains round it.

1 'Swiss' - in writing to his father who, two years out of three would take his sketching things to Switzerland for a tour, W. G. C. describes scenery in relation to what they both know of Switzerland, and the mechanics of painting in the more rugged conditions he is now facing.

2 'Dorrie'. W.G.C's wife - though at this period he addresses letters to her as Molly.

Abbot Hall

'Snæfell from Reykjavík' (*Saga-steads* 6) (13 August 1897)

W.G. Collingwood and Jón Stefánsson
travelling in Snæfellsnes

R.G. Collingwood Society

'Troll-karl', *Saga-steads* 62 (27 June 1897)

Snæfells nes

12 June to 2 July 1897

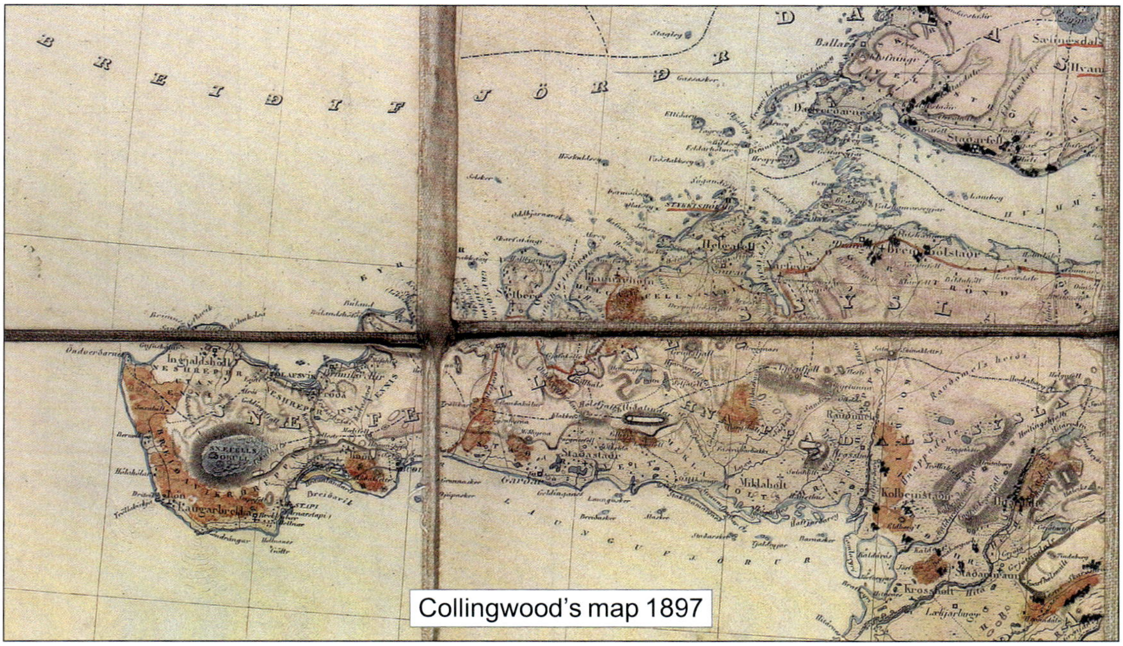

Collingwood's map 1897

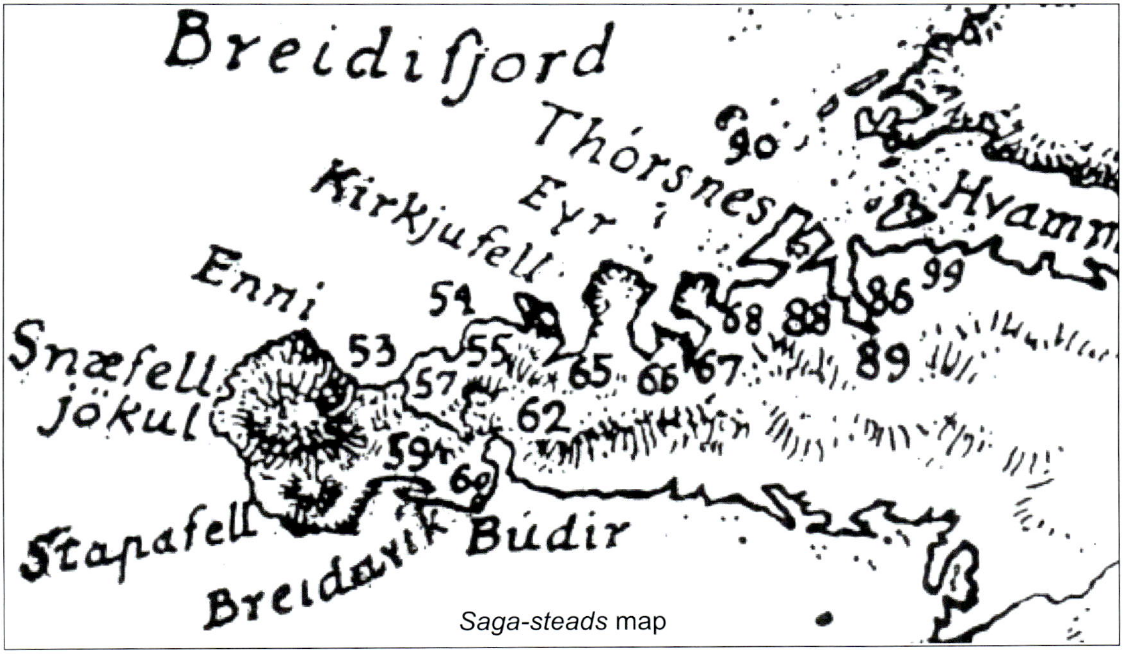

Saga-steads map

LETTERS FROM ICELAND No. 5

To: Dora Collingwood - aged 11

Dora at Lanehead

Abbot Hall

Hotel Stykkisholm, Stykkisholm, Iceland
day before Waterloo Day - I think - but* ? (i.e. 17 June)

My darlingest Dodie,

We are going away tomorrow morning and some day soon the 'Vesta' will come into the harbour and take letters. So that early next month you will get this, I hope - though it seems too far away for anybody to get anything. If you look at the map of Iceland, from Reykjavík you can follow our voyage on the Thyra across the Faxafjord and round Snaefellsnes and into the Breiðafjord. We meant to go all the way round the north-west coast to the middle of the north part, and there to begin our journey: but when we went aboard on Saturday night -

Oh, first I must tell you what we did at Reykjavík after posting to Mother. We had a tearing day of seeing more people, some of whom were very interesting: - and in the middle of the day took a little Relaxation by walking 2 miles out to the hot springs. Imagine one of the becks on the moor running the hot tap and the cold tap at once - or rather hot taps turned on out of the bank - through little drain holes: - and then washerwomen who tramp out those two miles, washing your clothes in this boiling water and rinsing them in the cold: - and a corrugated iron shed for them to finish the laundry work in - all alone in the middle of a big moor. It's awfully desolate - and far away, snowy mountains stand half round - and on the other side, the sea - with the houses of Reykjavík - tiny in the distance - silhouetting a low promontory.

Most of the houses are deadly ugly - not like Swiss, though built of wood: and mostly* of iron. When they build them they paint them, but never again. Desolate, neglected, disheartened - and all in the middle of a bleak cold windswept sea-coast. They said it was nice weather: it was like a fine - not mild day - in March: but this was all part of the cold 'snap' which they declare is unprecedented and rapidly passing: the sort of thing we have in May - and they in June, before settling down for the summer.

But one house which I didn't like at first I liked after wds. - outside the town, all of iron, very neat and new, a little tin box painted and glazed - with an emerald green field round it and marigolds as usual - and a garden with taties* just peeping – and a cowhouse and cows – and inside – the daddy – a big sturdy good sort of man, learned I suppose for he is head of the theological college – but not a bit like a parson – more like a country doctor: and nice mother and four* children – Dora, the youngest, who was greatly taken with the idea that I had a Dora too and wanted you to write to her. If you like to do so, she is ~~Froken~~ Miss Dora Bjarnarson – she will like better to be Miss – and Reykjavík, Iceland is address enough – a 2½d. stamp or penny postcard. She is about as big as Ursula – but her father will read her the letter.

Finally at Eleven at night – as they call it by courtesy here, we went by a little boat

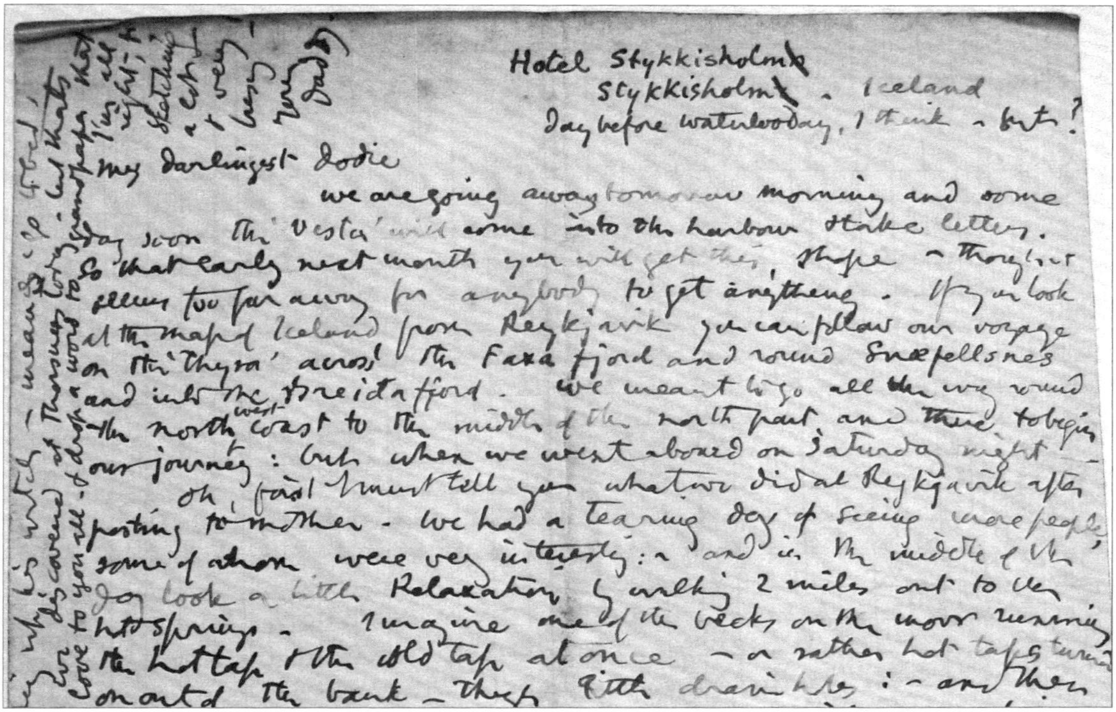
Hotel Stykkisholm
Stykkisholm . Iceland
Day before waterloo day, I think - but?

My darlingest Dodie

we are going away tomorrow morning and some day soon the 'Vesta' will come into the harbour & take letters. So that early next month you will get this, perhaps - though it seems too far away for anybody to get anything. If you look at the map of Iceland from Reykjavik you can follow our voyage on the 'Thyra' across the Faxa fjord and round Snæfellsnes and into the Breidafjord. We meant to go all the way round the north west coast to the middle of the north part, and there to begin our journey: but when we went aboard on Saturday night - oh, first I must tell you what we did at Reykjavik after posting to mother - we had a tearing day of seeing more people some of whom were very interesting: and in the middle of the day took a little Relaxation by walking 2 miles out to the hot springs. Imagine one of the becks on the moor running the hot tap & the cold tap at once - or rather hot taps turning on out of the bank - then little drains [illegible] : - and then

Abbot Hall

to the steamer which was crowded with people saying goodbye in pouring rain - and after watching them for an hour or more, we went to bed rather dismally. Next morning we rounded Snaefellsnes, and the snowy top was in cloud - a violent north wind blowing - as cold as it could be. The Yankee and the Frenchman were again our fellow-passengers - and the boat was crowded - and not very cosy - what it must have been second class I don't like to think; but a perfect black hole - with seasickness added - I'm afraid. The gale grew worse and worse as we passed cape after cape looming out of cloud over an angry white and green sea. At last we came to a lonely moon-shaped island - cliffs all round of vertical basalt - crowded with eider ducks; and in the middle of it - as in a coral reef - quiet water, and green fields, and a house or two - A boat came off with four people rowing - a man and a boy and a woman and a girl - pretty one too - and put a pilot on board. I asked the name of this island, and - you don't know what a thrill it gave me to hear it called Elliða-ey - however I dissembled the thrill that time, and we steered into the archipelago of rocks that make up the inner part of Breiðafjord - steep rocks - and skerries - and great basalt crags - and soft green holms, and big ones* and tiny points sticking into the water - or only reefs under the sealine - and wherever eiderducks can sit, there they are now building - and every downy nest's full of eggs - great green eggs that are very good to eat - only its against the law to sell them. People can give you them, you know, and I've eaten a lot - lived on them mostly here - as a change upon the aniseeded nastinesses that Danish cooks call French cookery.

So when we came into Stykkisholm harbour there was a Norwegian sailing ship in the place where we ought to be - and we had to lie outside. They said we couldn't get off until the wind went down - and that might be days; for there was cargo to land, and they couldn't do it in the storm. It was bitterly cold - every place was crammed - wet outside and nasty within. We had a lot of thinking what would happen if the ship was long delayed - or worse, stopped at the north cape by arctic ice, which a fishing boat reported. Next day (Monday) I was so dismal that I said I'd cut this ship - and so we came ashore about midday in a sailing boat - lovely swallow-flight of voyaging after the stinks and joggling of the steamer; - and up here to the 'Hotel', as it says outside.

Teresa Smith

'Lýsingr and Servant Girl in front of Theil's hotel'

I was a dismal wreck - not with sickness but with cold and crossness and upset; a couple of sailors - Captain and mate of the Norse sailing ship - seemed to take pity on me and gave me whisky, and invited us to sail with them to Dyrafjord - and then I went to bed and slept till dinnertime (about five) and then to bed again and slept 14 hours on end and woke next morning all right - But the weather wasn't.

It's a funny Hotel - over a shop in a wooden house with a portly landlord and landlady - he talks a few words of English - and their children come into our bedroom to see our things. We have meals with the family - real table d'hôte - and infinite politeness all round. Herr Theil pours you a little thimbleful of liqueur to begin with and you drink it to wish him good morning - then you have all sorts of sausagey things, cold, in slices on plates, and then you've coffee - and shake hands all round and you've done - that's breakfast. Before which the servant girl with Iceland costume* comes into your bedroom with coffee - and if you aren't awake, gives you a shake by the shoulder to wake you. Dinner is about five - you have soup - meat done any way but the plain* way - and (Oh - the soup, first day, was sweet soup: figure-toi chérie, sago boiled to gruel, sugar in it as much as possible, dried cherries and raisins blowed out in the boiling - I ate a full soup plate of it without winking.) And no pudding, but cheese and coffee and handshaking. There are short beds and eiderdown duvets, as in Switzerland, so that one's toes are always out at the end; but I've had good nights and one doesn't mind the oddness if one keeps warm and gets filled.

But the cold has been awful - I have all my clothes on - but the wind from the polar ice goes all through, when one is sketching out of doors - and riding! but I'll tell you that in turn.

First day we went off to Helgafell walking - that was the Holy fell where was a famous nunnery and monkery, and before that Gudrun lived there - the lady who was the prettiest in the land - and married four husbands - but never the right man after all. In very old age she died there and we found her grave shown by the children at the farm - a big heave in the turf, just outside the present churchyard - and while I sat sketching - came a long procession on horseback - parson first - coffin next, and all the neighbours, as in old times in Lakeland. They stopped at the Kirkgarth, and took the coffin into the church - and then began to dig the grave. Before I had done sketching Jonas of Helgafell, the farmer who keeps the church and owns* the farm - a sort of a Stalkery man[1], came up and bowed* to Dr Stefansson - and

Teresa Smith

'Jonas of Helgafell'

asked if he were Doctor Jón - and then, great rejoicings. Everybody knows* about us, because the newspaper had it in, on our arrival at Reykjavik. And so we couldn't escape - but had to come in to the best room - something like the boxroom at Gillhead[2] - all the rest like the very roughest cottage one sees: peat fire on floor, hole in top for smoke - quern-mill which 2 women turn - peat walls - Everything of the ancient type. We had all sorts of things to eat and drink - and then had to go to the funeral.

My dear - to go to see Gudrun's grave, and to see it out of the church window just at my elbow while they were doing the sort of meeting-service - droning hymns and long sermon and sobbing people - In the spot where Snorri the priest lived - through* the gate where Gudrun saw the ghost standing as she went to church - in the church (rebuilt of course) where she used to pray o'nights till she fell asleep and dreamed that an ancient witch rose up, and bade her begone - would have killed her 'but that I like thee better than most.' - All this was rather emotional, and too much for your daddy.

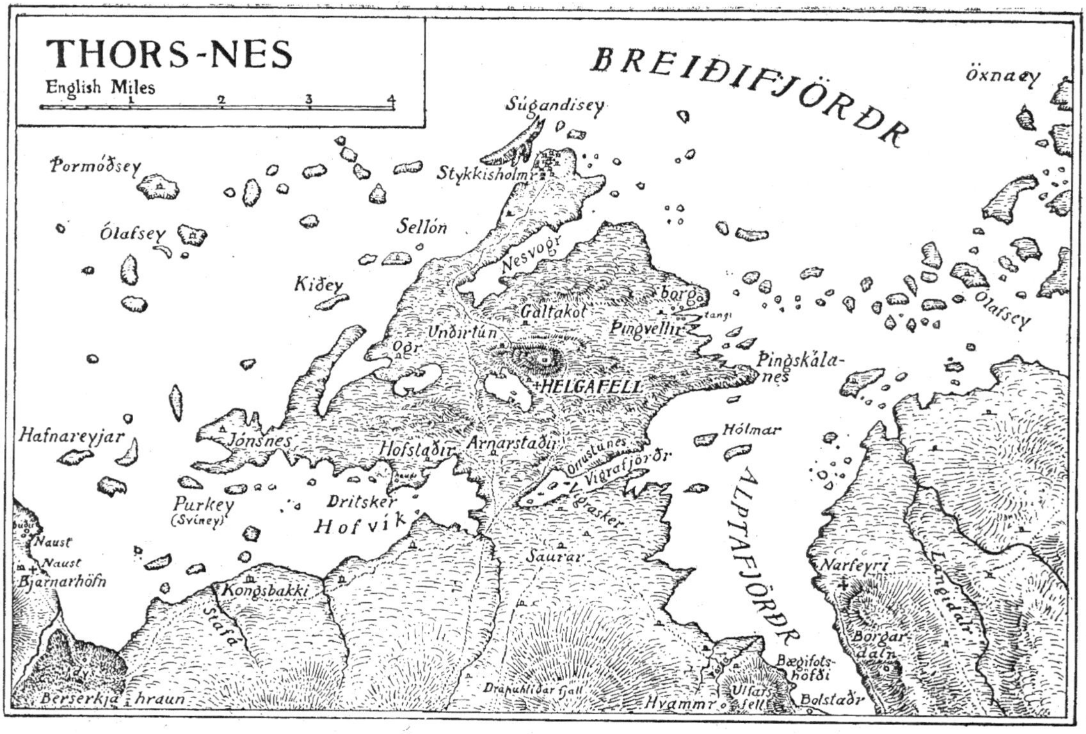

Saga-steads

Nevertheless, Gudrun herself thought it right to dig up the witch, and actually found a heathen interment under the church floor, with magic things in it. And will you believe it, your daddy went back next day and dug up Gudrun. I wouldn't have done it, but antiquaries have pooh-poohed the tradition; and I put her all back again, except some of the teeth and a bit of her skull bone - and a knife, and a bead - and I begged her pardon as nicely as I could and said I would write something to please her, and have her grave respected now that I know - as far as it is possible to know (I won't give you the argument here: that is for the Reyk. Soc. of Antiquaries to whom we'll give a paper) - that it is the next most important tomb in the world to Ilaria di Caretto's, that is the next most interesting lady's grave, to people like your daddy.

Teresa Smith

'Jonas' wife and child'

I got also Thor's hammer found last year at Helgafell, and some sketches of the place - in spite of cold and rain. Next place was the Thingvellir of Thorsness (not the great Thingvellir, but the one where Cormac and Bersi went - where the Thorstone is on which they offered human sacrifices). I drew the stone - and we saw the people of the farm, a nice blind man, and rosy cheeked girl - and fine servant lass who scrambled to the top of a house, up the green grass roof and stood on the top of the gable like a Greek Goddess and called to a far off labourer 'Koma heim' - when we wanted a man to put us over the water. While we were there a baby was born, and I said we were strangers and perhaps fairies, and it might bring the baby luck if we gave it presents - so we each gave a sort of halfcrown - and the rosy girl seemed mighty taken with the idea. We were there again today, riding: imagine your poor daddy trotted over the worst bits of the Old Man (the ground is the same) and terrified out of his wits, and shaken to bits. Somehow I stuck on - and got back all right - bitterly cold - to find an invitation to a party - which I use as good paper - and flatly decline, in order to write this letter. It's the apothecary and family - speaking a little French and playing 'The Virgin's Prayer'. We spent one evening there - and tonight* after supper called on the parson who is married to a sister of Mrs. Magnusson. People are awfully, dreadfully hospitable -and every farmer is hurt if you pass his house without spending an hour and taking coffee. They are all exceedingly slow - and I begin to see we can't do more than half what we should, simply because of the people.

Teresa Smith

'Window of guest chamber at Helgafell'

Teresa Smith

'Jonas' horse - the best in Snæfellsnes'

End) It's close on 12 - bright day - the landlord comes in winding up his watch - means 'go to bed' - so good night to you all. I haven't told you all the interesting things we discovered at Thorsness today - but that's mere* antiquities. Somebody will manage to read this perhaps - anyhow love to you all - and drop a word to grandpapa that I'm all right - and sketching a lot - and very busy -

your Daddy.

---

1 'a Stalkery man' - Christopher Stalker and family were farmers in Coniston, at this time at How Head a few hundred yards down the road from Lanehead. (Mentioned in works of John Ruskin as a shepherd.)

2 Gillhead - the Windermere fisherman's roadside cottage where the Collingwoods lived 1883-1891, a very modest home.

On the back of the paper is the printed heading 'Stykkisholms Apothek' - 'E. Möller' the date 17-VI-1897, and some lines that are to me illegible, but apparently the invitation addressed to Dr. Stefánsson, signed E. Möller.

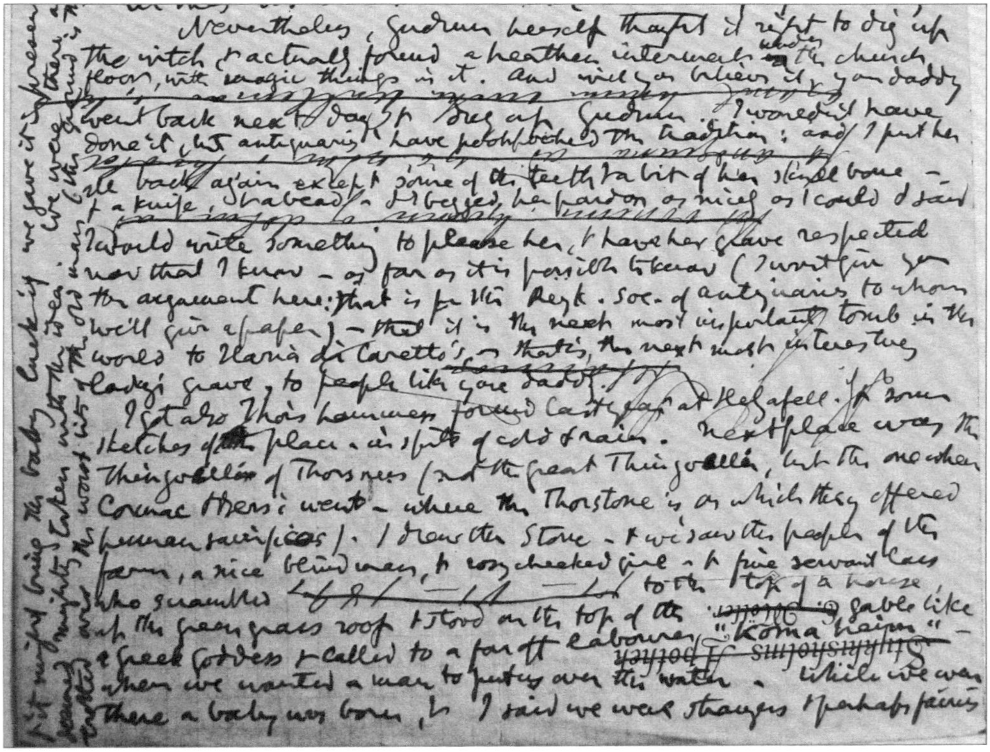

Nevertheless, Gudrun herself thought it right to dig up the witch & actually found a heathen interment under the church floor, with magic things in it. And will you believe it, your daddy went back next day to dig up Gudrun. I wouldn't have done it, but antiquaries have pooh-poohed the tradition; and I put her back again except some of the teeth & a bit of her skull bone — & a knife, & a bead. & I begged her pardon as nicely as I could & said I would write something to please her, & have her grave respected now that I know — as far as it is possible to know (I won't give you the argument here: that is for the Reyk. Soc. of antiquaries to whom we'll give a paper) — that it is the next most important tomb in the world to Maria di Caretto's, — that's, the next most interesting lady's grave, to people like your daddy. I got also Thor's hammer found casually at Helgafell. & some sketches of the place, in spite of cold & rain. Next place was the Thingvellir of Thorsness (not the great Thingvellir, but the one where Cormac Ogmundsson went) — where the Thorstone is on which they offered the human sacrifices. I drew the stone — & we saw the people of the farm, a nice blind man, & rosy cheeked girl & a fine servant lass who scrambled to the top of a house up the green grass roof & stood on the top of the gable like a Greek Goddess & called to a far off labourer "Koma heim" — when we wanted a man to put us over the water. While we were there a baby was born, & I said we were strangers & perhaps [illegible]

'Thor's hammer'

Abbot Hall

Abbot Hall

'Blótsteinn at Thorsness-thing' ('The Altar of Thor' *Saga-steads* 82) (15 June 1897)

LETTERS FROM ICELAND No. 6

To: Ursula Collingwood - aged 6

Ursula at Lanehead

Abbot Hall

Stykkisholm. last of June 1897.

My duckie Shursha,

This must be for you - as I have not written to you since we left - though I think Dr. Stefansson has. Behold our two ponies - both together costing less than £10 - long tailed and long maned and white - mine is called Flugnir, which means Flyer, 'cos he goes so fast, and Dr. Stefansson's is called Lysingr, which is as much as to say Whitey. They are both very nice and good, though. Flugnir tried to throw me yesterday when Lysingr was being taken away from him, and he didn't like parting. I had a Millstone round my neck, in the shape of two halves of a very big stone Thor's hammer discovered at Helgafell, - I'm taking it to give the Museum at Reykjavík, and had the two halves slung in a string round my neck, as I said, and the animile danced round and round, and kicked; and I felt as if I got very red in the face and then I whipped him: and then I threw the stones on the ground and whistled, which is the way Iceland ponies are made to whoa. He was all right in the end, and today the young lady of the hotel has ridden him, and says he is a very good pony indeed - Lysingr is at Helgafell having a rest for two days - Reason why? - Turn over and you'll hear.

Stykkisholm. last of June 1897.
My duckie Shursha - this must be for you as I have not written to you since we left. though I think Dr Stefansson has. Behold our two ponies - both together costing less than £10 - longtailed and longmaned and white - mine is called Flugnir, which means Flyer, 'cos he goes so fast, and Dr Stefansson's is called Lysingr, which is as much as to say Whitey. they are both very nice and good, though

Flugnir tried to throw me yesterday when Lysingr was being taken away from him, & he didn't like parting. I had a millstone round my neck, in the shape of two halves of a very big stone that's been discovered at Helgafell; I'm taking it to give the museum at Reykjavik, and had the two halves slung in a string round my neck, as I said, and the animile danced round & round, & kicked; and I felt as if I got very red in the face, and then I whipped him: and then I threw the stones on the ground & whistled, which is the way Iceland ponies are made to whoa. He was all right in the end, & today the young lady of the hotel has ridden him, & says he is a very good pony indeed - Lysingr is at Helgafell having a rest for two days - Reason why? - Turn over & you'll hear.

Abbot Hall

We went away from this place ten days ago, or so; with Stefan of Bjarnarhöfn's horses - to meet him at Kongsbakki - you'll not care about the names, but Molly can get down the Ere Dwellers and turn them up in the index and see what things happened there. Kongsbakki is King's bank - don't know what king: any way parish council was held there that day - Friday - and we rode with Jonas of Helgafell (Jonas not Jones) the farmer who helped us to dig up Gudrun. He lent me his horse which he wanted to sell me - it was splendid and went like lightning: but I thought it was too dear, so I didn't buy it; and now the people here say mine is better, and went better today when they tried both together. At Kongsbakki we waited and I sketched and saw the hand loom in the farm where the farmer showed me how they wove wadmaal, and gave us coffee as usual - and when the council was done (they were interested to hear I went to parish council at home too) we rode to Hraun (Lava) where was a jolly little turf and wood house with nice people and pretty little girl like Shursha, whom I photographed, - and they made the best coffee I have tasted. Everybody gives coffee - but you mustn't pay - only you must give something to the children. They are all like that. You have to take what they give, and not pay, but give something to somebody - so it's rather more

Abbot Hall

'Flugnir and Lýsingr'

expensive than paying! And the odd thing is that it is not respectable to go on foot. You may be in rags - most people are; and exceeding dirty, and pick your teeth with your fingers and talk with your mouth full and all sorts of bad manners; but you must ride, or nobody will take you in. That is the custom of the country - and a very inconvenient one. But all Icelanders ride very well indeed. Tiny boys and girls ride barebacked ponies at full gallop over rocks and moors up and down all sorts of steep places and through rivers - everywhere; and the best roads in these parts are worse than the Walna Scar road in its worst places. At Hraun we saw the sheepfold the Berserks built, and the house where they were killed, in a bath; - and then rode by the path they made - one of the best hereabouts, through a vast field of lava which came out of a volcano which was burning about 900 years ago, and then stopped. The lava is all a waste of ugly blocks, and heaps of rough stone, with moss and lichen growing in the crannies but nothing else. Most of the mountains are proper mountains like ours; rather bigger and there is a great deal of snow on them still; but here and there is a red volcanic cone; and a lava field filling a valley, ugly to behold, but curious in its way. When we got to Bjarnarhöfn (Bjorn's haven) we were entertained by the farmer Stefan and I slept well for I was very tired and cold. It was still bitter weather, like winter; and next morning was wet, and we went to see the ship docks or boathouses in which Bjorn from Norway, the brother of Queen Auð of Dublin (who also stayed here) kept his boats. At last we set off, with Stefan to guide us, over a pass called Trollahals (Troll-hause) like Styhead pass with fine waterfalls, and snowy peaks. It was awfully steep going down and several times I thought I should go over my pony's neck - but I didn't. At the bottom of the pass we had a good gallop

Abbot Hall

'The Berserks' Road and Cairn' (*Saga-steads* 69) (18 June 1897)

over a grassy plain at the head of Kolgrafafjord - with Eyri in the distance, where the Ere dwellers lived; and I got a good sketch in the evening light. There was a ghost at Eyri last winter - it rode the roof, and banged the walls, and burst in the door, and came up to the bed-room and frightened everybody terribly. The farmer, whom we met coming from parish council (another one, at Dr. Stefansson's father's) was away - and I think it was a sham ghost meant to frighten the farmer's wife; but nobody here will believe that; because it behaved like the ghost in Gretti's saga, which proves, they think, that it was real.

Well - we got to Grundarfjord in the evening. Dr. Stefansson's father - whose name is Stefan Danielsson, was surprised to see us, and had just finished his council, of which he is chairman - so there was a great running about to get us things to eat and drink. The house is a tiny wood and peat cottage on the shore of the sea, with big mountains all round. The mistress was away on a visit. The master was a tall thin man with a moustache, exactly like a Swiss, and talking a little French, learnt from French sailors who used to come fishing to his fjord. He owns a lot of land - chiefly bog and fell - and has sheep and cows and horses, but no garden - and they farm in the Irish way - you don't know what that is - but it comes to this - doing as little as possible. Of the people, I should fancy they are Icelandic Martindales[1] (that is what Mother will understand) and they seem pleased with everything they have, and proud of all they are. We had brandy and whisky and port, and beer, and milk and coffee and halibut and potatoes, and I slept on the sofa in a room where everybody had been smoking and spitting, but I didn't mind a bit. Next day was Sunday and I was extremely tired and cold; they brought two children of the house - the servants (three women and two men) live with the people and keep their children in the house - and asked me draw their portraits - as I had already done a child at Bjarnarhöfn. I struggled through and then went ill - and had to go to bed in the farmer's bed where I stayed two days, with fever and a sort of dysentery - I was very ill as I thought, and I couldn't eat anything but hot milk, nor do anything at all but try to get warm under immense eiderdown quilts. There are lots of eiderducks - and I saw a mother duck teaching its ducklings to swim - she takes them on her back into the water and dives, and then they <u>have</u> to. It's a very sensible way. Well - on Tuesday I crept out and drew the waterfall, which is magnificent, and saw the midnight sunset from a hill behind the house, with glorious crimson and gold clouds - that was my Jubilee Day, and a very pleasant one - feeling I was better, and thinking about Lanehead, and the doings at Coniston: and we drank the Queen's health in tiny glasses of aniseed brandy: and determined to get forward next day. I was not quite well, but the weather was better, and I got another horse, and the farmer went with us to show the way. I thought I should never stick on - I felt so weak: but somehow I did and we went round the fjord in bright sunshine with grand snow mountains glittering above, and blue sea beyond. We passed Bulandshöfdi, a narrow path on a steep slope high above the sea, where Mr. Magnusson had to half carry Morris who was frightened[2]: and they thought I was going to be afraid: but one doesn't live among

Teresa Smith

'Head of Hraunsfjord - waterfalls at foot of Trollaháls'

R.G. Collingwood Society

'Grundarfoss', *Saga-steads* 64 (22 June 1897)

mountains to be frightened at them, and I sat down in the worst part to make a sketch. Then we came to Máfahlið (Mewlithe) a lovely place among green fields and waterfalls and snow mountains, like an alpine farm: with curious carved wooden front to the house. There we had coffee, and then set off past Katla the witch's Holt, to Froðá; which is on the brink of a beautiful river like all that Mr. Ruskin describes the Scotch rivers to be. We meant to stay the night there, but a child was ill in the house: and so, though it was late, we went on to Olafsvík, between firth and fell, and by lots of the prettiest waterfalls they make in fairy land: with ferns (beech fern and oak fern especially) and flowers lovely in the evening sun. At Olafsvík we stayed the night with the parson, Síra Helgi (they call them Sir, as they did once in England, and everybody is known by his christian name) a school friend of Dr. Stefánsson's, and next day it was really warm and nice and like summer. We went back to Froðá, and got two boys to show us the way up to the

Teresa Smith

'Cottages, Ólafsvík'

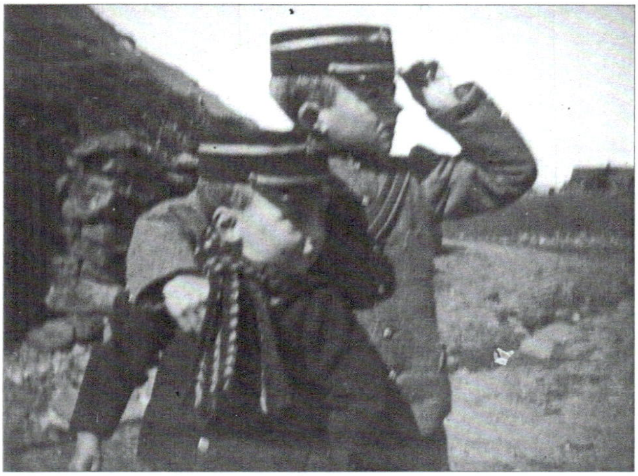
Teresa Smith

'Síra Helga's boys'- Ólafsvík'

place where Björn the Broadwicker's champion jumped the river when he was chased by Snorri and his men - and the cave where he stayed three days in a snowstorm, and then we went on alone over the Kambskarð, a very high pass, with snow through which we had to lead our horses, and steep descent to Bjorn's house (the ruins of it) at Kambr. We had to ride through wide marshes, and another lava field, and got about midnight to Buðir, to the house of a Mr Saemundsson, a friend of Mr. Magnusson's. He was away, but his sister got up, and made us very cosy in nice clean beds in a pretty room. Buðir is a lovely place by the sea, looking south, in full view of Snaefellsjökull, a sort of Mont Blanc, which I painted in its midnight effect while they were making our beds; fine colour with green fields in front & *marsh marigolds in plenty among the grass. At Buðir we stayed three nights; and dug out the tomb of Asmund who was buried in a ship. This grave has never been found before, until we discovered it; and oddly enough a lawsuit is now going on between the two

Abbot Hall

'Snæfellsjökul from Kambsskarð' (*Saga-steads* 52) (24 June 1897)

Þjóðminjasafn Íslands, Ívar Brynjólfsson

'Búðaróss' 25 June 1897

Teresa Smith

Búðaós on 3 September 2006

statesmen[3] whose boundary is defined in a charter as passing through Asmunds howe. It will be interesting to see whether they accept our diggings as legal evidence to settle the case. I haven't time or room to tell of a long night ride - much longer than we meant it to be - to Stapi, to see basalt caves - and I was too tired and cross to see them after all - but sulked and sketched a wonderful effect of Buddha's rays and a rainbow over the sea, and the midnight view of Snaefell. We got home very tired at 4 in the morning. Next day we crossed a still higher pass, called Arnardalsskarð - Eagle dales scarth - with a man to guide us up - under tremendous crags and snow, and on the edges of steep gills. They all advised us not to attempt it, because it was too awful. But I find that Icelanders are afraid of mountains though they live in them; they never climb them, but keep to the valleys. We were the first to cross this pass in this year, with horses, though a man had crossed on foot. We had to go through many snow drifts and drag our ponies along like this: -

Abbot Hall

Ponies in the snow

and coming down there was no path at all, but we had to find the way through a steep and wild valley choked with snow. I got my horse down with a deal of coaxing, and no damage - but the other one had a fall and burst his girth, and cut his foot. However we rode into Grundarfjord again about 10, and Dr. Stefansson's father was quite astonished that we had crossed Arnardalsskarð alone, neither of us in the least knowing the way - one thing that helped was the pony I rode named Skjoni, who had crossed before, and seemed in some places to know what to do: though he was all the worse for that in the bad snow patches; but when we came to the dreary wet valley bottoms he could pick a path from hummock to hummock in a wonderful manner. Meanwhile Dr. Stefansson's father had found us the ponies we now have, and on them we set off next day, after I had painted the portrait of the house for him with three horses and himself in front of it (I did a house also for Kjartan, a man at Buðir who helped us to dig, and a big picture of Snaefell in oil for Miss Saemundsson who paints in oil in the - Danish manner) - and we went back over Trollahals alone, and through another part of the Berserk's lavafield, and after hours and hours of riding the poor Lysingr who had been over Arnardalsskarð the day before, and to Stapi the night before that, and so on, got very tired, and we couldn't get to Stykkisholm - but wearily dragged as far as Helgafell and knocked up Jonas, who came out in his shirt, and gave us milk to drink, and put us into a little bed, in which I lay for an hour with my knees out of it, and very uncomfortable as I always am from the bites of the animiles [WGC spells it this way when they are a nuisance] in which this country abounds: then I got out and dressed and slept on two hard chairs, and slept very well. Next day was wet, but we went to Hofstadr where the great Thor's temple was which Thorstein went to see (Robin can

Abbot Hall

Buddha's Rays, Arnarstapi (26 June 1897)

Abbot Hall

Snæfellsjökull from Arnardalsskarð (27 June 1897)

Abbot Hall

Descent of Arnardalsskarð (*Saga-steads* 63) (27 June 1897)

R.G. Collingwood Society

'Hraunsfjord', *Saga-steads* 67 28 June 1897

tell you) and saw a nice family in a new house which the farmer has just built all by himself - wooden `bathstofa' sort of gable roofed attic with beds along the side - the main living and sleeping room of all these people - with little in it except a clock and a spinning wheel. I drew the place - and we went back to Helgafell, where we were promised a good dinner of <u>steak</u> - which turned out to be liver, very hard: but it didn't matter for we were hungry. Then we had to wait 2 hours until Flugnir could be found - and arrived here between 10 and 11. We are staying two days to refit - Dr. S. to write up notes for next journey and to have his horse rested, and I to work up the sixty sketches I have made in this trip - we hear there is a boat going to Reykjavík on Sunday which will take all superfluous luggage, and this letter - the luggage to Reykjavík and the letter I hope to Coniston with dearest love to you all from your Daddy.

PS. for Molly - I couldn't write before, because we have been where there is no post. I am quite well; weather much better. 1 o'clock, going to bed.

I hope this letter is not overweight - but I don't happen to have other paper. I wish I could get news of you, but it's over 100 miles to Reykjavík, and there is so much to do we can't hurry forward and back. Everybody here underestimates time, money and distance - just like me.

July 1. Finished my sketches, and had a picnic on an* island with a lot of people who sang songs and I sketched. Tomorrow early we are to start to the north east parts. I don't know when I can get letters. We may be a month before we reach Reykjavík: but I hope and trust you are all well and comfortable. I think I am acclimatized now, and expect to get on capitally. I will write when I can but there are few post places. Let Grandpapa know that I'm all right

July 2. 9 am. just packing to start - fine warm weather and all very well. - Best love to you all. W.G.C.

---

1 'Martindales' — A Lake Country farming family known to the Collingwoods - 'statesmen' and proud of it - their daughter Christina was from time to time nursemaid to the children.

2 Eiríkr Magnússon acted as escort to William Morris in Iceland in 1871.

3 'Statesmen' - W.G.C. here uses the word in its specialised sense - in Cumberland and Westmorland - to mean yeoman (or owner-occupier of a farm) with the obligation to serve in border defence when required.

Góður gestur - An Honoured Guest

by **Ingi Hans Jónsson**

Travels with the son of the head of the Council of the Township of Grundarfjörður

Translated from *Fólkið, Fjöllin, Fjörðurinn* by Ida Talling
The People , the Mountains, the Fjord

Part 2: Articles on the history of Eyrarsveit, pages 9 - 25.
Eyrbyggjar-hollvinasamtök Grundarfjarðar (2001)

In the summer of 1897 a noteworthy Englishman, William Gershom Collingwood, visited Iceland. He was a well-educated philosopher and fine arts connoisseur, with a great interest in archaeology and history. Collingwood, born in Liverpool on 6 August 1854, was an excellent scholar and artist. Through his art he became interested in the inheritance of Scandinavian culture found in many places in the Lake District in England. Through his acquaintance with one of the most beloved English poets, William Morris, he became interested in the Icelandic Sagas. Morris was a great admirer of the Sagas, which he got to know from Icelandic scholars in Oxford and Cambridge, Professor Guðbrandur Vigfússon, and librarian Eiríkur Magnússon. Morris and Eiríkur were together translating the Icelandic Sagas, and Eiríkur and Collingwood became acquainted. Another intellectual, who quickly joined this group of learned men, was Dr. Jón Stefánsson, son of the head of the council for Grundarfjörður village. Many things encouraged Collingwood to travel to Iceland and he decided to make Dr. Stefánsson his guide. This expedition can be followed in a splendid book, *Fegurð Íslands* (Reykjavík: Örn og Örlygur, 1988) or 'The Beauty of Iceland'. It contains 163 of Collingwood's paintings and also many photographs and engravings. Most of the paintings are in the state ownership of Iceland [in the National Museum], but some are in private hands. Here, therefore, are only the travels of Dr. Jón Stefánsson and W.G. Collingwood on Snæfellsnes, and the paintings which we have found with the relatives of Dr. Jón, which have not previously been published.

In the *Eyrbyggja* Region

After a short stay in Reykjavík, the two of them took the post ship *Thyra* to Stykkishólmur and came alongside Elliðaey on the 13 June 1897. There they had to wait for a while, because the ship could not land at once in Stykkishólmur harbour. Collingwood was an impatient man, and did not feel like waiting on *Thyra*, so he had the company rowed ashore in a boat on the 14 June, and they settled in the hotel there. They noticed that the name of the hotel was just The Hotel, as if it were the only one in the world. They spent the next few days in Stykkishólmur, travelled up to Þórsnes, examined saga-steads and Collingwood painted some well-known pictures. One might, on the other hand wonder why no pictures by

Stefán Jónsson (Daníelsson), the last Chairman of Grundarfjörður council

him of Stykkishólmur exist. He must have painted quite a few pictures there, as Stykkishólmur had become quite a town, one of few in Iceland. They left Stykkishólmur on the 19 June, for the time being, and travelled towards the rural district of Helgafell, stopping at Kóngsbakki, Hraun and Bjarnarhöfn. Then they went to Hraunsfjörður over Tröllaháls and down into Eyrarbotn. Many pictures are known from this trip, but in the evening, when they approached Grund, they must have gone a bit up Mön, because one of the most recently discovered pictures is of the colourful sunset. This picture must have been painted on 19 June, as in a letter [number 6] he sent to his family he 'got a good sketch in the evening light'.

In Grundarfjörður

He spent the next three days at Grund, tired and ill as mentioned in the letter. He was able to move around a bit, and he seems here to have painted some of the following pictures here. In a letter from Collingwood to his daughter, Ursula, he describes his travel around Snæfellsnes and his stay in Grundarfjörður [see Letter no.6]. He met Dr Jón Stefánsson's father, Stefán Daníelsson, and ate and drank 'brandy [note: Brennivín] and whisky and port, and beer, and milk and coffee and halibut and potatoes'. The next day, Sunday, he was rather ill but he recovered to go out on the Jubilee day to draw and then toast the Queen's health with anis flavoured brandy.

They start again

The letter continues by describing Collingwood's trip to Ólafsvík, south around the Jökulháls, and his stay at Búðir and the archaeological investigations in Breiðuvík and finally the return trip to Grundarfjörður over Arnardalsskarð mountain pass. I have tried to date this trip from this information and the two travellers seem to have arrived in Grundarfjörður in the evening of 19 June, and stayed there till they started their trip to Ólafsvík in the morning of 23 June. They

'Hvol' (*Saga-steads* 122) July 12, 1897

'Grundarfoss' - Collingwood painted three pictures of Grundarfoss 22 June 1897

Buddha's Rays, Arnarstapi (see another version on p.56) (26 June1897)

Stefán Daníelsson by his turf-roofed house in Grund, where they stayed (23 June 1897)

stayed one night with the parish minister and the next day they went over Jökulháls to Búðir. In Búðir they stayed from the evening of 24 June, and roamed around Breiðuvík the next 2 days and then returned to Grundarfjörður on 27 June over Arnardalsskarð mountain pass. The trip over the pass is very amusingly described in his letter [no. 6].

Back in Grundarfjörður

Stefán, head of the Council, was, as could be expected, very surprised to hear about the travellers' perilous journey and gave them a great welcome. They set off again after he had painted a portrait of him with his ponies in front of his house.

Family contributions to the story

In the following article, Guðmundur Steinbach describes the discovery of some more pictures by W.G. Collingwood from Snæfellsnes. It was a great good fortune for us in Grundarfjörður to discover these pictures and publish them in *Eyrbyggja*. An exciting task remains to find out if there are any more; with Guðmundur Steinbach's help. The splendid book, *Fegurð Íslands* contains 38 paintings from Snæfellsnes [Eds: there are also six in Abbot Hall, Kendal]. Of the eight pictures found by Guðmundur, five are around Grundarfjörður, one is labelled Geirþjófsfjörður, [Eds: one is of Arnarstapi]. We know that when Collingwood arrived back in Stykkishólmur, after his trip described above, he finished some 60 pictures. It is also possible that he gave some pictures as presents during his travels, so more paintings may be found.

Ingi Hans Jónsson

Myndir Collingwoods - Collingwood's Paintings in Denmark

by **Guðmundur K. Steinbach M.Sc., electrical engineer**

In early summer 2000 my cousin, Anne Klauber, an eye-doctor, wrote to say she was attending a Scandinavian doctors' conference in Reykjavík that summer and would very much like to use the opportunity to get to know her Icelandic family. She is the grandchild of my late grandfather's brother, Stefán Stefánsson, a doctor in Aars on Jutland, and the daughter of Ingibjörg Gowers Lund, a doctor in Copenhagen, born in 1905 who had died the previous autumn aged 95. My grandfather was Óli Steinbach (Stefánsson), a dentist in Ísafjörður, so Anne and I are second cousins. I had only met her once before at her mother Ingibjörg's house. Anne worked for many summers in Greenland and had often had a stop-over in Iceland with no time to visit family and country. Her sister, Susan Misfelt, also worked in Greenland for many years. She is also a doctor, married to Jens Misfelt, head physician in Greenland, and they often came to Iceland. This made us very happy and at the end of the conference my daughter Auðbjörg Steinbach and her husband, Kristján Loftsson, invited the family to a midday meal. Besides Anne, there were also present nearly all the descendants of Stefán (Jónsson) Daníelsson, council chief in Eyrarsveit and his wife, Jacobina Árnardóttir Þorsteinsson. After the family gathering, Anne, my wife Kamilla Guðbrandsdóttir, and I started our journey round Snæfellsnes.

The origins

We drove around Hvalfjörður, had coffee with Jóhannes at Borg hunting lodge, which my friend was preparing for its opening. We again passed Arnarstapi, in front of the glacier and stopped at a few places. Then to the Vaðstakkaheiði and photographs were taken of some walls without a roof of the house where our forefather, Þorsteinn Runólfsson, was born, though he felt at home with men from Grundarfjörður. On we went, and after a short stop in Ólafsvik, we arrived in

'Kirkjufell' (*Saga-steads* 65) (23 June 1897)

Kvöldroðinn, taken from Grundarmön, looking over the country round Setberg - note the fishing vessels and the people on the shore (22 June 1897)

Krossnes where our great-grandfather and great-grandmother, Arni Þorsteinsson and Christense Benedichte Andreasdóttir Steinbach had lived, with yet more photographs of walls without roofs.

Our next stopping place was Grundarfjörður and we knocked on the door of the parish pastor, séra Karl V. Matthíasson, and borrowed the key to Setberg church, containing the tombstones of Árni and Christense. Many people from Grundarfjörður have without doubt seen these. The next and most important place was Grund. Photographs were taken to compare with the Collingwood paintings we knew about. Here again were more walls without roofs on the house in which our grandfather grew up. We had with us a computer-scanned copy of Collingwood's picture of the house, with our great-grandfather Stefán standing by the door. Everything agreed.

The last place we stopped was Bjarnarhöfn, where our cousin Óli Steinbach the younger is buried. Though it was close to midnight, Hildibrandur Bjarnarson, the farmer, was still about and my cousin was offered pickled shark and brennivín. She disliked both of these! We arrived in Reykjavík in the middle of the night and we were all happy after a successful trip. Anne left the country the next day.

Back to Denmark

Our story returns to Denmark because the photographs from Setberg church did not show the inscriptions on the tombstones and I was again contacted. I telephoned séra Karl who promised to help. After some time I telephoned again and he said: 'With me is a gentleman who can quickly solve your riddle, Ingi Hans Jónsson and you can contact him through me'. And séra Karl was indeed right. To continue my request, Ingi Hans and I talked. After telling me all about himself, he wanted

Grundarfoss (22 June 1897)

to know all about me. At last we talked about Dr. Jón Stefánsson, my grandfather's brother and Collingwood's guide on his travels around the country. Among other things, Ingi Hans asked me if I knew the whereabouts of Collingwood's painting over the Grundarkamburinn towards Kirkjufell, found in Jón Stefánsson's book *Úti í heimi*. I should say so. The painting was hanging on the wall of the living-room of my aunt Ingibjörg in Copenhagen, along with more paintings. There was also a painting of the farm Grund with another aunt of mine, Guðrún Hvidberg Jensen, Ingibjörg's sister in her home in Copenhagen. Ingi Hans considered this important information, and asked if I could get photographs of these. I then contacted my aunt Anne and she was quite sure that her husband, Valdemar Klauber, a doctor but also a computer and photographic enthusiast, could easily do this. A few days later I received by computer the seven paintings in her mother, Ingibjörg's, ownership and I sent them at once along to Ingi Hans. The painting of Grund was missing and I therefore contacted still another doctor of the family Jesper Hvidberg Hansen, the son of Guðrún and he answered quickly. A few days later it arrived in the same way as the others.

Unsolved questions

Many comments can be made about these paintings and many more questions asked. How did my grandfather's brother Stefán come to own them and thus his family? Did Dr. Stefánsson own these and give them to his brother when he visited from London, where he lived for 50 years. His sister, Kristin Blount, also lived there. Are there more paintings? One thing is sure, that Ingibjörg only had these eight paintings. Does Guðrún own more paintings? She is very old, born in 1906 and deteriorating. But it is only a year since she gave up cycling to the coop 'Brugsen'. Could there be some paintings with the heirs of their brother, Árni Stefánsson, another doctor in Brondstrup in Jutland, now widely scattered? Did Kristin own any, and where could they be? Collingwood often visited her and Jón was a frequent visitor. My two cousins are quite sure, but they cannot prove it, that Collingwood stayed with their grandfather, Stefán. Did he pay for his stay with a picture? He did so here, with sketched portraits of children. Collingwood was both quick and painstaking. Did my grandfather Óli or his sister Kristensa, married to Kristján Stefánsson, forester at Vöglum, have any paintings? Where could they be? We know they met. All this and more will be investigated in the future. It will take a longer time than available to be included in this publication now. I should indeed have realized earlier the importance of this cultural treasure for this local community to which I belong. During the last 15 to 20 years, many of my cousins have come to Iceland and more often than not, they have gone on a pilgrimage to Grundarfjörður.

Guðmundur K. Steinbach

Digging up Guðrún:
The Grave of Guðrún Ósvífrsdóttir by Jón Stefánsson
from ***Árbók hins Íslenzka Fornleifafélags* (1899)**

Translated by Ida Talling

In the old churchyard at Helgafell, which can just be spotted in the homefield north of the present churchyard, there is a large grave, much overgrown with grass. This grave has long been attributed to Guðrún Ósvífrsdóttir and called Guðrún's tomb both by people in Helgafell and in the Helgafellssveit district. This agrees well with *Laxdæla* which says Guðrún is buried at Helgafell[1]. And in June 1897 W.G. Collingwood and I examined [rannsakaði] the grave, with the permission of the farmer of Helgafell, and found possible clues to the grave being of a female from the beginning of the 11th century.

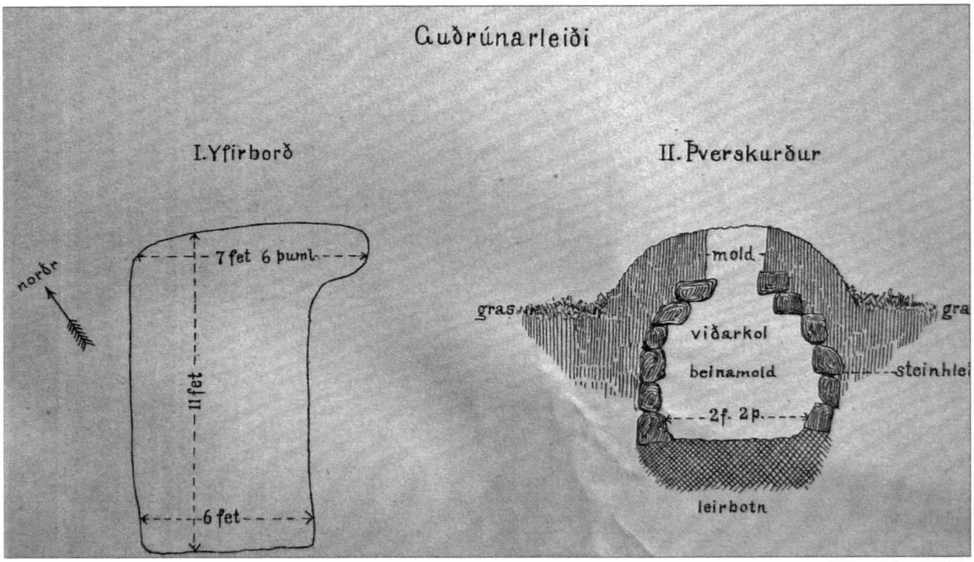

The grave is 11' long, 7' 6" wide at the northern end and 6' wide at the south end. The height above the surrounding soil line is about 2', and the depth down to the bottom is 4' 10". It points in a north east and south west direction, as shown in the drawing with this article. The grave was piled up all around and much charcoal was found there, similar to finds in mounds from the saga age, which prevents decay. Quite a lot of bone fragments were found under the charcoal and in the north end some small teeth (female?), and fibres from the remains of the skull lining. At the bottom of the grave in the north end was some iron rust, a piece of iron, bent, battered, very likely a harness knife, and a small beach pebble. In the middle of the grave, about 8" from the bottom of the grave, there was a small stone with many glistening facets. It could possibly have been from a rosary belonging to a nun, but there was no hole in it. It also appeared as if at some stage the grave had been disturbed, possibly by sheep looking for shelter. This might explain why no more was found of the rosary or costly pieces, as nuns were not buried with gold and precious things.

1 *Laxdæla* Chap. 78: 'Guðrún died at Helgafell and rests there. She was the first nun in Iceland and hermit'; Chap 76: 'She was the first woman to learn the psalter in Iceland'.

The stone wall and the finds in the grave point to an origin from the tenth and eleventh century as far as one can deduce from graves which certainly date from that time. *Laxdæla* tells us where Guðrún Ósvífrsdóttir is buried. Legends and traditions attribute the grave to her. The grave is from her time and according to what was found, it should be a female grave. This all points in the same direction: *Laxdæla*, traditional storytelling, historical tales from later times, the grave building and what was found in the grave. This all strongly points to the possibility that a most distinguished woman from the saga age, Guðrún Ósvífrsdóttir, was buried here. I would like to point out that we put back everything we found in the grave in the same fold and posture as found, with the exception of a few things which will be sent to the Antiquarian Museum of Iceland.

R.G. Collingwood Society

'The church etc from the side of Helgafell', *Saga-steads* 80 (15 June 1897)

From ***A Pilgrimage to the Saga-steads of Iceland***, p.92.

'It was at Helgafell that Guðrún gave the most famous answer to her son, describing her lovers, and - 'I did the worst to him I loved the most.' Here she died in extreme old age. Her grave is doubtfully pointed out - a mound of turf, 11 feet by 5, lying N.E. and S.W. just outside the modern churchyard (seen with two figures standing by it in the view from Helgafell, plate 80). The present writers excavated it and found an undoubtedly ancient tomb, built of masonry; the upper courses overhanging so as to form a vault. There was the layer of copsewood charcoal and the small gravel which characterises graves of the Viking age in Iceland, below which were fragments of bone and grave earth. It seemed to have been disturbed at some distant period and there were no valuable relics; perhaps none should be expected in a Christian grave. Fragments of iron and a banded bead were all that a careful examination disclosed.'

Stykkishólmur to Vatnsdalur
2 to 18 July 1897

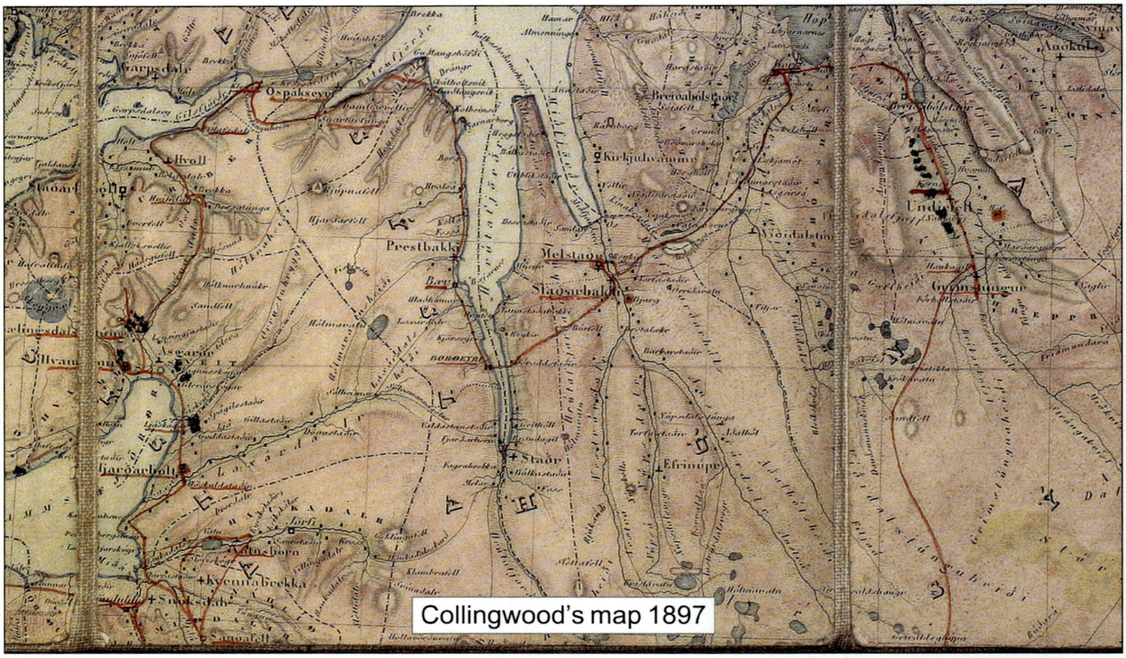

Collingwood's map 1897

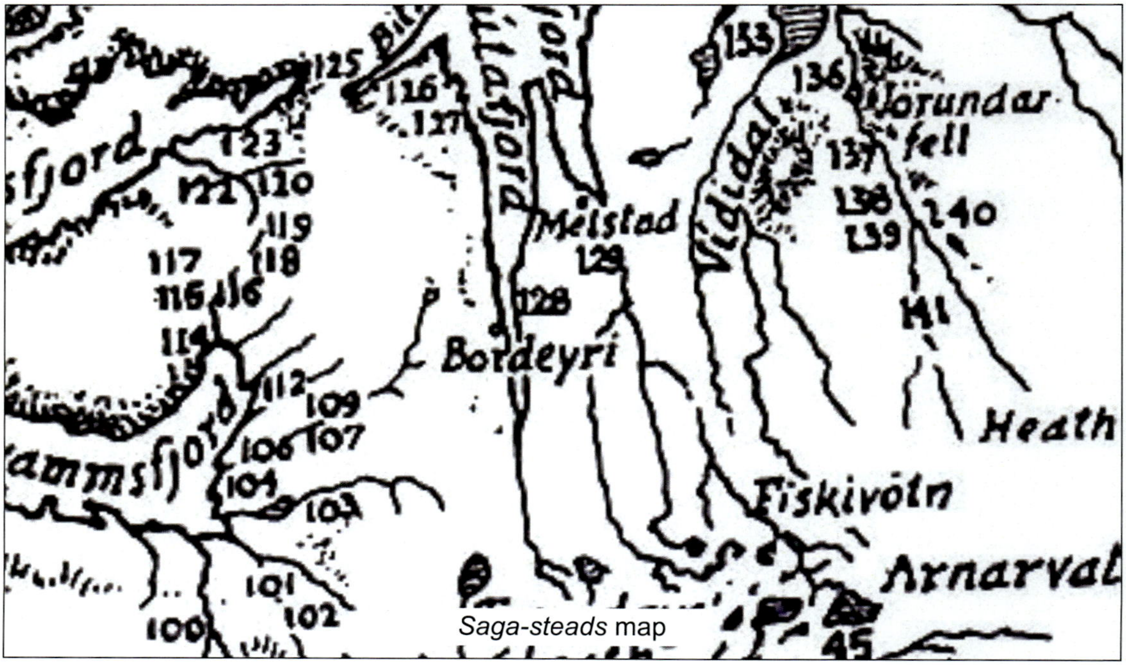

Saga-steads map

LETTERS FROM ICELAND No. 7

To: Mrs. Collingwood.

'Mother' by Barbara Collingwood

Abbot Hall

Hjarðarholt.
Thursday, July 8, 1897

My darlingest Molly,

There seems to be a chance of sending a letter to Reykjavik to catch the boat sailing for Leith in the middle of the month. We have just got newspapers giving European news - mightily little of it - of rather more than three weeks ago - how president Faure was shot at, and how the Turks and Greeks can't be brought to terms. But as I didn't know of this opportunity, your letters will be still lying at Reykjavik for weeks - though I weary for news of you.

This is Herdholt where Olaf Peacock had his great house with the carvings and the tapestries - and flocks and herds by the hundred - and Kjartan was brought up here - Kjartan who didn't marry Gudrun. Opposite, and across the ravine of the river, is Höskuldsstaðir - Hoskulds stead - on a round green hill with a beck running by it - winding along 2 sides of it & the river at the other side. There is the green bank where the Irish princess who was bondwoman, and made believe to be dumb, was overheard talking to her baby and so discovered to be a Queen in disguise: - and on the top of the hill the remains of the enormous hall which Hoskuld built to entertain over a thousand people, all at once; and down below is where Kjartan swam in the Laxa: - you will see the story in Morris's Lovers of Gudrun. Morris was here just 25 years ago - stayed several days with his party (Magnússon, Faulkner, and another) in tents - and it is well+ remembered by the parson, Síra Jón, who lives here - a sort of Mr. Ellwood[1] - whose son manages the farm on improved principles - with a cart, and a separator - and one or 2 other things not known to the usual Icelandic baer. The church is just outside - a mangy, dilapidated - no, there are no stones in it, so it can't be that - but forlorn and neglected shanty - in which service is held once a month, because people won't come, the parson says. Religion seems to be exceedingly unpopular in Iceland, parsons especially - and they don't take any steps to make matters better. (Of course, I only can tell what I've seen so far: - I hear of a popular preacher who is a Unitarian - and preaches on poetry, and tells his trips abroad from the pulpit: he, being popular, can't be put down, and the bishop had to contrive some way of reconciling his heterodoxy with right Lutheranism: that of course is what bishops are for.) But everything is forlorn and neglected. All this valley and the next valleys and the shore of the fjord used to be full of wood - not perhaps timber, but copse: - I saw big branches, as big as my wrist, at a farm near here called 'Sawrey', pulled out of the bog. But at Sawrey and elsewhere are bloomeries - and they have used up every atom of the wood long ago, and the whole place is as bare as the top of the Old Man. Then they strip the turf to build their huts and walls - and great spaces are not even decently grassed over.

\+ The only thing I gather about him is that the party were quarrelling about Probate and Income Tax all the time, and they caught salmon in the river and threw away the tinned things they had brought to eat. (W.G.C.'s footnote).

The people at this place (the parson being also farmer) and the Sysselman at Sauðafell are doing better work; but the whole lot are more prejudiced and ignorant than even our good neighbours at home. - So it seems to me. - They are half Irish, and their manners, and appearance, and dirt, and content in it, are wholly so. Consequently, the Herdholt of Olaf Peacock is no more to be seen than the Greenodd of Thorstein of the Mere. It is a wide open bare valley, with snowy mountains in the distance, cold in a rainy sunless sky, and patches of snow on the long lines of moorland, still waiting for summer. Everybody declares it is unprecedented - this cold weather. Everybody declares it is going to mend at 12 o'clock, or tomorrow - and much warmer now, while I shiver in 2 pairs of breeches and an overcoat. But the impression is very different from the rich Alpine picturesqueness of the Eyrbyggja country which we have left: and for all its beauty must depend on its meadow land and river banks. I want to get down and draw the Laxá in its ravine, but it has been too wet, all the morning, for more than a sketch of the house and church with a buttercup meadow in front, and a study of the distant mountains from the window. If you think of Longsleddale and Kentmere, without any trees or walls, you get an idea of the scenery of the Dalir - the Dales - round Hvammsfjord - it is Westmorland in early spring, waiting for the Croppers and the Wakefields to wake it up.

We left Stykkisholm on a fine morning, as I wrote last, and rode to Helgafell: where Jonas made a last series of attempts to get us to buy his horse: and then to a farm where the bóndi and his boy took us to see ruins of the house of Thorolf Baegifots, the

R.G. Collingwood Society

'Horðadalr' 4 July 1897

Teresa Smith

'Lest (pony train) near Ólafsvík'

onelegged man in Eyrbyggja who turned into such an awful ghost, when he died, that the whole valley was deserted, and is still so. We saw also his grave, in which he wouldn't stay, and followed the route by which his body was dragged on a sledge by oxen over a hill to a headland on Alptarjord - Swanfirth - where they tucked him into a new cairn and built a wall across the promontory to keep him in - which (like the Borrowdale Gowk story) was no good: so they had to burn him: and then a cow drank some of the ashes and her calf turned into a devil bull - and we saw the place where it went into the keld in the bog. Then we went round the firth to a quaint lap* of green land under great crags, where a lady built a house across the path so that everybody had to call and be treated: that is still the custom - and there is not a house but expects one to turn in and drink coffee: a dilatory custom and monotonous, and to me irksome, for there are always lice as well: and they all come to me - I suppose because I am fond of animals. This lady's place is called Borgardale - Borrowdale - and the next valley is Langdale, and the next is Little Langdale. Alptafjord is called from the Swans that flock there. I saw only 2, but elsewhere many: and their 'singing' in the distance sounds exactly like a pack of foxhounds: rather monotonous and strident. We stayed that night at Narfeyri, with a farmer, over 70, who looked 50, and his wife a cousin of Dr. Jón's father - a very young looking and pleasant looking woman. I slept on a sofa rather than 2 in a bed - and next morning walked back to Borgardale to draw - and then we started on a weary long ride over moors by almost untraceable paths, against a bitter wind, hoping to reach Sauðafell. At last about midnight, in the rain, a man came out in his shirt and gave us directions about crossing a river, which we couldn't manage after all. We wandered among bogs for an hour in the wet and went back to the farm - I was very cross - and glad to see some-body riding along - whom we accosted and he turned out to be the farmer of Blönduhlið, coming back from Olafsvík - a 2 long days' journey - with three pack horses carrying dried fish. We asked him the way, and he showed us - but it seemed dismally long, and so he took us to his house and knocked people up, and made us beds on the floors at one in the morning, or thereabouts (time is rather vague here.) Next day he took us up the valley, Hörðadalr, to an old saga place, Tunga, and showed us the rock - like the Pillar of Ennerdale, - where eagles build, and told us how an eagle had carried a child up there, and the mother ran after it all the way and fell dead at the foot of the 'Stone of Sorrow.' He wanted me to try to climb it, as Englishmen do everything - but it seemed that it was very difficult, and only once had been done: and I was tired.

The day came out bright after a good deal of rain, in which I found the old holdall anything but waterproof: - and I sketched a little, and we met a man who showed us the way to Sauðafell - Southerfell - to which we had been invited by the Sysselman - let's say sheriff, that is king's officer, factotum, magistrate, taxgatherer, auctioneer, general boss of the county. The sysselman is the only official, except the parson and the doctor: everybody else is farmer. This one, Björn Bjarnarson, is a clever, energetic and popular man,

Teresa Smith

'Sysselman at Sauðafell, and Church'

who lives in a turf house and farms his land, with great ideas of improvement - going to build a glass house for plants - yet unknown in the land - and introducing separators and carts, and getting the farmers to level their infinitely humpy meadows and so forth. He has two oil pictures - a ship among icebergs, and a Norway fjord, and he knows artists in Denmark and reads English books, but can't talk English. His wife is very nice, and they have five children, brought up to run about the fell, and all sturdy rough youngsters. I did a rather good portrait of Anna: a little crop headed girl, more like 6 than 4, which was her age, with a big decided mouth and grey eyes, like them all. But I was sick and ill and couldn't eat or do much. Dr. Jón was full of explanations, and decided that it was because they had been digging a cellar, in which an ancient sewer was found - dating from the Sturlungs'* time (sewers being unknown in later and more degenerate Iceland) - and the miasma, don't you see? Anyhow I don't stand roughing it as well as I could wish, and I wanted to be at home. Everything tastes so nasty - I don't know how they manage it - that one has to be very hungry and well to eat. I suppose they like their own tastes - and perhaps that was why Dr. Jón ate so little at Lanehead. We stayed three nights at Sauðafell sleeping in a comfortable attic which was scrubbed out for us on the second day - a compliment: for generally the floors are such that I don't take off boots till I sit on the edge of the bed, ready to whisk up my feet. All this doesn't matter to people brought up in it - they seem healthy - and surprised when they heard that our children had baths every morning and evening. And the Sysselman thinks England must be a very sink in iniquity - from what he has read: and his wife has never seen such dirty people as in Leith, where she has been on landing from the ship to Copenhagen. So you see we are all prejudiced - which didn't prevent them being very kind, and my being grateful. One afternoon was spent in riding to Haukadalr to see the ruins of Eric the Red's house (the discoverer of Greenland). It was very sunny, but cold wind: and next day, yesterday, I could only just stick on the horse when we came away. The Sysselman took us to the holm where Cormac fought his first duel - and then to the rock where Snorri and Gudrun sat and talked - and then we went on to Hrútstaðir, a saga place, ruins of house and temple - which I sketched also: though it was cold and dull. And so we rode over a brink into Laxardale - stopping at Saurar - Sawrey - for hot milk, at a very poor miserable hovel with a very sweet-faced middle aged woman in it, and some sturdy children. By and by we

Abbot Hall

'Sauðafell, outhouse'

'Hrutsstaðir' (*Saga-steads* 104) 7 July 1897

came to Höskuldsstaðir of which I have told you, and stopped for coffee and sketching, and inspection of ruins: and as they told us the time at Hjarðarholt was 1½ hour faster than at other places we came on, in order to catch them before bedtime. Síra Jón, the parson is father of the Iceland doctor whom I saw in London in spring. He doesn't talk English or French or Latin - so I am dumb and can only say No, thank you. We sat an hour and a half, on arriving, doing the usual preliminary talk: then had supper, and then I was shown into a cosy little box of a room with a clean bed -. and a looking glass, but nothing to clean one's teeth with - no tumbler, I mean. People don't clean teeth here: they all have very good teeth, and say it comes of eating rikling, dried fish - which is all very well if you begin early, but I find it hard to bite and indigistible to swallow. They have always an Eiderdown thing on the bed and a sheet about as big as a towel. The Eiderdown is awfully hot - so I sleep under my coat: and try not to wriggle in the night, except when I'm bitten; and then I get up, and start fresh. At present it is looking like steady rain. They propose excursions, but I explain that I can't draw in the wet. I see nothing for it but to stay in, and work up sketches. The sysselman has come and has been holding a Thing, public meeting - sort of 'court' - everybody in the parish comes on horseback, and pays taxes, and does general business. They talk of a new road between here and Sauðafell - but I don't see why. There is practically none now: but nobody ever comes along except the people who know every bog hole and wath: and a stray traveller always asks for a guide. A greater venture is the sysselman's plan of getting a little steamer to ply in the fjord which would bring all sorts of conveniences within reach: but the parson deplores the steamboat travelling, which he says enervates the young people - when he was a boy he used to go to school at

R.G. Collingwood Society

'The Ford of Laxá, and Höskuldsstaðir', *Saga-steads* 108 (7 July 1897)

Reykjavik from East Iceland, three weeks journey, on a pony: of course he went home only once a year: and seems to have had larks and adventures on the way. But certainly the country is in no sense open to tourists. It is ridiculous to dream of it, until all sorts of alterations are made. The mere fact of being always guest at a little house is, to an English tourist, most embarrassing and boring: and neither when one is at one's entertainer's, nor on the road, is there freedom and leisure to make decent drawings. No doubt when the Sun shines again I shall be thinking more cheerfully - and I hope the cheerfulness will go into the sketches. At the moment I write as it comes - and I will write again when there is another chance. But we get on slowly, and if rain stops us, I don't know how long we may be. Dearest love to you all from your very loving, W.G. Collingwood.

I meant to send something for August Nothing Much[2]- but I'm afraid I have no brains nor time - I hope you get on all right with the Sec. work,[3] and that Brantwood is all well. Remember me to Mary and Ellen and Ethel and Shaw.

1 'Mr. Ellwood' - the Rev. T. Ellwood M.A., Rector of Torver 1864-1911.

2 *Nothing Much* - the monthly magazine produced by the Collingwood children, edited by Dora.

3 'Sec. work' - secretarial work for John Ruskin - letter writing which had been left in Mrs. Collingwood's hands.

LETTERS FROM ICELAND No. 8

To: Mrs. Collingwood.

Reykjavík.
July 29. 1897.

My darlingest Molly,

We got here last night and asked for letters - only 2 were found: but this morning we got some more, so that in all I have one from my father - one from Ruthie[1] - one from Mr Ellwood - and from Lanehead yours of June 27, July 1, July 7, July 13, with 2 from Dora, 2 from Barbara, one from Robin and one from Ursula. All were very welcome and I thank you very much for them and for the paints. I am puzzled at getting no letter of earlier date than June 27: and no news about The Book of Coniston[2] or anything about how the Coniston Bank business was managed - except that they are furnishing it[3]. But these things I shall hear when I come -

When I come is what I don't know till this letter has to be closed. The Laura sails tonight - the Vesta on the 3rd. If we go by either, we must leave important places unvisited and half our work unfinished - hoping for another time, which may never come. It is hard work, and I dare say I shall never care to buckle to it again: so that it would be a good job to work it off now. I have made about 200 sketches in colour - not without value as sketches - and with very great value as record of places much talked of and little visited: and if the series were completed by going to Njal's country, and the north west, and Gretti's Drangey, it would be a great achievement. Of course we've spent all our money. My companion's estimates were hopelessly under the mark: but being here I find that another £15 would bring us home - and he has gone to see if he can raise it. In that case we'd go south for a fortnight - then catch the Thyra on the 14th. and go round the north into all the fjords; make a clean sweep of all important sites, and reach Leith August 28th. I think it worth while, if we can raise the money: for I must have an exhn. of the sketches and many will sell - and the book will be bought by Icelanders, if nobody else. Everywhere people have expressed the greatest interest both in the project and in the sketches I have shown them. They are all anxious to have Iceland illustrated - and here's their chance.

But all this waits to see whether he can raise the wind: - meanwhile I'll begin a short story of how we did since I wrote at Hjarðarholt.

It was wet there, and I was pulled down with cough and other things: but at last we got off, with one of the priest's sons who has invented a new machine for sharpening scythes, and wanted information about English machine shops. I wished I had Herbert Severn[4] there to tell him things. He took us to Ljarskógr on the Hvammsfjorð, where is a bloomery just like those at home (I got a bit of slag.) and a hoftoft* (temple ruin) and kirkjubrú, church bridge, a 'bridge' they say, - I suggest 'covered gallery' - from house to church along which were bells - and when the gentlemen* went to church all the bells rang so that they heard them over the fjorð (look it out in *Grettir*). Of course this is all ruins now. Thence to Hvammr* - where Queen Auð settled finally, after coming from Dublin: a charming Borrowdale-like valley, with the fjord like a lake at one end of it - and hundreds of wild swans on the shore. We saw an eagle quite close, being baffled away by a lot of peewits (I think but forget exactly) - <u>quite close</u>, as we rode along the beach. Birds are so tame that in one place a raven sat still on a rock not three yards from us as we rode past and stopped to look at him. I would have Kodaked him but it was too late in the evening: and puffins came to me the other day as I sat among their nests sketching, and they pottered and puffined about as though I were just an old woman like themselves; as the ald body said till the curate. - At Hvammr lives Síra Kjartan, a tall, thin, shaved priest with ideas of improving agriculture - and an energetic wife who arrived during our stay after riding all night from Reykjavík with a doll for one child and a trumpet for another in the bag at the back of her horse. The rain had flooded the rivers, after we passed them; and she was nearly carried away in the floods - riding alone - but nobody thought it extraordinary. Síra Kjartan lugged us up in the wet to a very big waterfall, but I couldn't make much of it: it was too elaborate for hurried sketching in rain and wind. This has been the case with many places: they needed three days work, where I could give only a halfhour's knock-in, and that with much discomfort.

We left Hvammr with a farmer who offered to show us the way for the day: and as usual riding through showers and over floods and mires and rocks we got into a valley called Saelingsdalr where is a farm under grand crags, and near hot springs called Laugar (Bathstead) where Gudrún was born and brought up. The hot springs used to be nicely walled and covered and seated, but scree has slipped down and destroyed the old buildings - though the water still wells out and steams into the air. Nobody thinks of putting pipes to these springs, and the poor women tramp to them with the washing, and slop away in the open air - cold sleet and boiling water on the hill-side - a bad sort of laundry. Up the dale is the place where Bolli was killed while Gudrún was washing the clothes (see the poem). We couldn't find the exact spot, as we might have done for it is known - but I drew the general look of the hillside, and we went to Saelingsdalstunga where Snorri Godi lived after he swapped farms with Gudrún. It is now a picturesque but a poor place - 2 farms near together; on one we had coffee - and a curious Italian looking little girl astonished me by her difference from the usual flaxen-haired child. We went - all the farm people too - and saw the ancient churchyard with Snorri's grave - which I drew, but badly, being in a crowd - and then we started for a long pass through Svinadalr.

I think I'll continue the story to Dora, in reply to her 2 letters. You understand, this is the first chance of posting - for all this while and you'll see that we have been far indeed. With dearest love, your W.G.C.

---

1 W.G.C.'s sister (Sophia) Ruth Collingwood (1856-1937).

2 The Preface to this little guide book was written in May 1897.

3 Coniston Bank (now Thurston) less than half a mile from Brantwood, was bought by Mrs. Severn earlier in 1897.

4 Herbert Severn (1882-1935) the youngest of the family, was mechanically minded and an engineer.

LETTERS FROM ICELAND No. 9

To: Dora Collingwood - aged 11

Dora at Lanehead

Abbot Hall

Reykjavík.
July 29. 1897.

Darling Dora,

I have 2 letters to thank you for, and a long story to tell - a bit to each is the best way: and as my pen is bad, and ink German, you must read, or get read, this letter any way you can: and if it amuses you it will be more than I can expect. The story is just one of riding tired horses, painting hurried sketches, eating nasty food (and little of it) and sleeping in close and stuffy holes: with just enough mountains and rocky shore, and just enough ancient history, to make it all worth going through. All these places are not much in themselves - though they are savage and wild mountain scenery, halfway between the Lake District in winter and Switzerland in its higher and bleaker parts: but every place was once the home of some interesting person or the scene of a fight, or the exact spot where some great event happened - so that one forgets for a while that one is wet and cold and hungry and miserable, in thinking of the people who were there so long ago, and about whom fine books have been made, telling true stories of their doings. In Svinadal - which is a sort of long Tilberthwaite without any trees (I don't mean the gill, but the valley) - is the place where one of the greatest of the ancient people was killed. News came that he was travelling home: Gudrun, who loved him - and he loved her - but they had been parted by one mishap and another: - Gudrun got up early and woke her brother - saying that Kjartan would be coming through Svinadal with hardly any men. What's that to me, said he - Well, said she, if I were a man, and Kjartan had done such injury and insult to my family as he has to yours, I should know what to do. In the end her brothers rode off and sat in a gill to wait for him. Bolli, who had been Kjartan's foster brother, and now had married Gudrun, said he wouldn't go on such a business. Then, said she, I will be your wife no longer: - because she hated Kjartan all the more, that she really loved him in her heart. So in this gill they sat behind a rock, and Bolli sat up on a little height to watch for his friend. We found the gill and sat in the rocks - and on the bank, just as they did. Bye and bye the brothers thought Bolli meant to warn Kjartan, and so they crept out and began to lark with Bolli, and finally pulled him down the bank by his legs and kept him behind the rocks. At last Kjartan came riding - and suddenly, over the edge, there they were, with their swords ready to kill him. He leapt off his horse, set his back to a stone - (you'll see the stone in my picture) and fought a long while. Bolli did nothing till several were killed - and then, at last, what with Gudrun's brother's taunts, and Kjartan's calling on him - he took up his sword as Kjartan threw his away, and stood still: and Bolli gave his friend the death wound and then held him in his arms till he died.

Well, my dear, we found the spot, all just as it had happened - and for the first time

Abbot Hall

'Hafragil,where Kjartan fell', *Saga-steads* 118 11 July 1897

R.G. Collingwood Society

these thousand years, drew it just as it was. People have cried over Kjartan's death many a time, but nobody ever drew the place before, or thought out exactly how it all happened.

Then we rode up the dale and down the dale on the other side of the pass, in the darkening evening to the place where Bersi lived, who married the lady that Cormac loved -

'The Cairn on Valafall' (12 July 1897)

and the spot where Vali was killed by Bersi when he was very old and the little boy Halldor. I think I found Vali's grave in a cairn of stones. We came down to a big river and splashed about in it to get across and ask for lodging - 2 men were riding over and we followed them: and one turned out to be Dr. J. Stefansson's brother, a student who had come for the summer to a farm nearby called Hvítadalr. So we went with him - and were well received by the owner, who has only this summer come into the property. He has been many years in America, as a sheep[1] man in Dakota, where there are many Icelandic emigrants: and he talks English quite well, with an American accent. His house and ways are much neater and better than most. Indeed the only clean and tidy Icelanders are those who have lived out of Iceland for a good while. We saw another next day at Olafsdal - Torfi, who has a sort of farming school, and gets forty young men to learn farming. He has a very fine new wooden house, just like a Swiss hotel in a Swiss valley, and I slept for once in a bedroom all to myself, with a clean floor, and several windows just as if I was in a nice Swiss hotel. Torfi was for a good while in Scotland at Peterhead, and so he talks English. He made us very cosy, but we arrived late, and had to start early - and it was very stormy weather: so we did not have much chance of enjoying the comforts of Olafsdal. You'll find the Gilsfjorð on the map, with a narrow isthmus between it and another fjord called Bitra. This isthmus connects all the big peninsula of the North West with the rest of Iceland, and it looks a mere hairsbreadth in the map, but it is really all big mountain land, a long and difficult piece of country to cross. They said the road was plain - the main post road - but my dear, the best bit of it is worse than the path from the Low Water quarries to the top of the Old Man. We stopped in pouring rain at a farm called Kleifar (Claife) where an old old fellow in blue spectacles tottered out, and it seemed a shame to let him stand at the door. Finally he

Abbot Hall

'Garpsdalr from Olafsdalr' (*Saga-steads* 124) 12 July 1897

brought us in and gave us coffee and cakes, as usual - and proposed to take us over the pass. I thought he meant to send a boy, but No! this old chap toddled out and climbed on his horse and talked the whole way up - winding in and out of great crags, great awful crags that completely close in the dale, and down which a tremendous waterfall comes. You wind up and up until the waterfall is as far beneath you as it was above you: and then wind up into clouds and among snow patches: and then follow the merest track through* rocks and bogs and over rivers - the track leading to the edge and you shove your pony in among the boulders, and everything* seems swimmy for a bit, and you tuck your feet up on the horses back and try to sit still, and then he's scrambling up the bank on the other side. And so we got to a cairn on the top, and the old man got down from his horse, and extracted a snuff horn from somewhere in his dripping and sodden clothes, and said the rest was all down and clear: - and we gave him 2 kroner (a krone is a little over a shilling) and he wouldn't have more than one, which was the proper price for a guide - and then he'd accept the extra krone as a present and so on. He got aboard his horse, and vanished into the fog, and we had a long and dismal ride down through wet and wind.

This pass is more like the mountain part in 'The Glittering Plain'[2] than any other description I know. It's a nightmare of mountains and mist: one huge shape follows another, alike and different - and river after river, snow after snow, bog after bog, rock after rock - till you get quite confused and almost frightened. I can quite understand now why people used to be afraid of mountains, in the days when there were no roads through them and no hotels among them. They are very different in Iceland from the tamed Alps.

We got down wet through to Snartatunga where Steinvör Slimankles (in Cormac) lived - and a man there said he was going over the pass we had crossed but would turn back with us, and put us up and dry our clothes. He was Gudmunði of Ospakseyri - a place that was once a robbers hold, conquered by Snorri Godi: now a comfortable farm where we got into the farmers clothes, and ate an Icelandic supper of rye bread and butter and various smoked and soured meats, with lots of milk. I slept on the floor and made them very astonished by preferring a rug to the eiderdown duvet.

Well, I can't get more in: but I'll continue in my next to Barbara.

Your loving Daddy.

---

1 '*Sheep* man in Dakota' - his pen was bad, and the word is S. H. blot P. and could be equally 'ship' or 'shop' I have chosen 'sheep' as more likely?

2 *The Story of the Glittering Plain* - by William Morris, Kelmscott Press 1891.

LETTERS FROM ICELAND No. 10

To: Barbara Collingwood - aged 10

'Barbara' by W.G.C.

Abbot Hall

Reykjavík.
July 29. 1897

My duckie Bab.

Thank you ever so much for your two letters. Did I thank Dora for hers? But I have them and like them. Glad to hear you can ride and play chess. There you beat me, for I can't play chess. But I think six weeks riding every day and all day over all sorts of places on various sorts of ponies makes one less afraid than before of tumbling off. I did tumble off twice - right over the horse's head, when he went into holes in bogs: but not so as to hurt myself. And I have had splendid wild gallops on fast ponies, and long tiresome jog trots on ponies that were like smallish carthorses, and rides round precipices, as if one rode in the water gutters at the top of the house, only more so: and down and up hills steeper than the Old Man. And I'm not smashed yet: nor shaken to a jelly. So that's all right.

'Nothing much' and 'A little more' will be an excitement for me when I get home, and I shall be glad to read in it all about the Jubilee. Have you made any jokes about Jub and Jubilee? I am amused at people's saying 'You, you', like Robin: they spell it 'Jú jú', but its the same. When there is a pause in conversation somebody says reflectively 'Yow, - Oh yow!' (they spell that já) and then another says 'You, you.' And that fills up the time, and they take snuff, until something else turns up to talk about. On the whole the people are much like North English or Lowland Scotch Farming folk: with a bit of Irish in them sometimes: and no gentlefolk at all. They are civil and polite in a way, and don't get cross; rather quakerish in that: but they never can tell the real time, or the distance, or how much things

Abbot Hall

'Thambardalr & Bitra' (*Saga-steads* 126) 14 July 1897

cost, or any plain facts about plain things: and that is rather worrying when you want to know where you are.

Well, I told Dora how we got to Óspakseyri - and next day we crawled on slow horses round Bitra, past Thambardalr* where Bersi killed the people that had carried off Steinvor: and over a high headland came down upon Hrútafjord - a very long narrow inlet of the sea: with fanciful rocks on the shore, very picturesque and pretty with cottages among them, and flowers, and birds, all in the late afternoon light, and with deep blue and white mountains

Abbot Hall

'Sysselman S.E.Sverrison at Bær'

Abbot Hall

'Bær'

Abbot Hall

'Bær'

Abbot Hall

'Bær'

in the background. But our horses were tired: we suspected the people of the last place must have used them while we were resting. They went very slowly - and at last, quite late we reached a big new iron house, called Baer, and saw the master of it - the Sysselman or officer, sheriff or whatever you may call him, in a blue uniform with brass buttons, walking about in a field. When he came he took us in and gave us a good supper, and nice beds, and sent us away next day very pleased. This day had been fine, after much bad weather, and after that for about a week we had fine hot weather: so hot you can't imagine except by remembering that there are no trees and no shady places: so that every bit of sunshine burns. We rode to Borðeyri trotting nicely along: and there were received by Mr. Riis, who keeps the shop. I tried to buy some underclothes for a change, but they hadn't any: so we got chocolate and tobacco and Dr Stefánsson got a sort of collar that lasts for ever, and is washed with a sponge. Only he didn't put it on, but put it in his bag and strapped it on his horse - and when he opened it - lo and behold it was torn in two - which didn't prevent his wearing it for some weeks, dodged up with pins somehow. He might as well have gone without - for nobody wears a collar out of the town except on Sundays: even the clergymen don't, but go about in flannel shirts like raggamuffins. Mr Riis lent us his boat and we sailed over the fjord - sending the horses round with a man. But I think the hot day tired them, for they went very slowly afterwards and crawled over the mountain towards Melstadr (Mel) where Cormac lived and where we meant to stay. We got no farther than Staðarbakki to the house of a clergyman whose children have a nurse who has been in America and talks

Abbot Hall

'Borðeyri'

Abbot Hall

'Pier, Borðeyri'

Teresa Smith

'Dr.J.Stefánsson and Kerra Riis at Borðeyri'

English. She surprised me by coming up when I was sketching with 'Would you like to come in to supper, sir?' It was a fine sunset - sea and distant snowmountains, and broad river winding in the valley, and next day was bright and hot. We saw Melstadr - and then went on a road, a made road, to Viðidal, a valley with very pretty mountains; opposite which is a farm called Borg, from a sort of castle near it. The farmer was away, but his wife took us in and a delightful little boy named Christopher took us up to the castle. Imagine a sort of rock cup, standing high on hills, formed of basalt - not a volcanic crater, but a ring of rocks; all built up with walls of masonry: and inside ruins of houses where outlaws once lived. I sketched it all sorts of ways - and the farm people were delighted at the pictures of the 'poor (dear) Borgarvirki'. Late in the evening of the 2nd day as they were all looking at my pictures I began to sketch the children, and surprised them by knocking off portraits, ever so quick. I made a good one of Christopher and another of his mother. Indeed I have left a great number of portraits all about the place: for in several houses they asked me to draw the children, and in some I did it to amuse them, or to please the parents who had been kind to us. At Borg the eldest boy is called Willie. His father, when he was young, ran away from home, and stayed with a seal catcher - there are

Abbot Hall

'Melstad and Reykir' (*Saga-steads* 130) (16 July 1897)

Abbot Hall

'Pjetur Kristofersson of Borg'

Abbot Hall

'Kristofer Pjetursson'

lots of seals here - and when a certain English gentleman came shooting, this lad Peter did clever things with his gun and his horse, and Mr Hogarth said that if he came to Scotland he would look after him. So Peter found his way to Aberdeen, and sat with his trunk in the street, knowing not a word of English, until Mr Hogarth came by, and took him up and kept him for years and sent him to school; and now he is one of the richest farmers in Iceland. He wants Willie to get into an office in Liverpool, and I promised that I would do what I could for him when the time came.

R.G. Collingwood Society

'Borgarvirki, south west end', *Saga-steads* 131 (17 July 1897)

Abbot Hall

'Borgarvirki; north east end', *Saga-steads* 132 (17 July 1897)

R.G. Collingwood Society

Abbot Hall

'Borgarvirki; interior', *Saga-steads* 134 (17 July 1897)

R.G. Collingwood Society

Teresa Smith

'Farm servant at Borg'

Here they gave us splendid curds and cream, and I slept in a pretty little clean wooden house all to myself. Mr. Peter came with us next day up the Vatnsdal (Wattsdal they call it) - lake and mountains - and a saga about the Watsdale folk all to themselves. He even went ahead to tell the next house that we were coming: and all was ready when we got there in the bright sunset. After supper I sketched the waterfall and valley - and the Sysselman of the place - a very jolly young man, and the young farmer and his sister sang songs in three parts to the guitar - which was very pretty. We engaged a guide and horses for 12 next day to start over a long and difficult mountain pass - and so went to cosy beds at Kornsá, very well pleased. Now I've filled Bab's sheet, and sign myself her Loving Dad.

Abbot Hall

'Jörundarfell from Bay' (17 July 1897)

Vatnsdalur to Reykjavík

18 to 28 July 1897

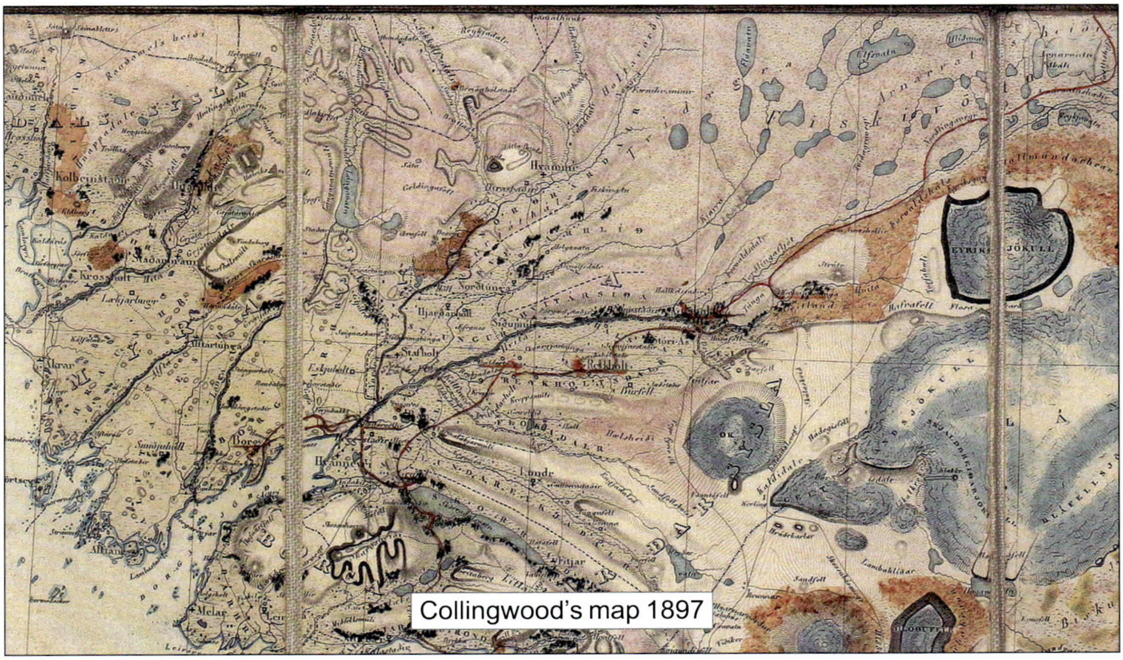

Collingwood's map 1897

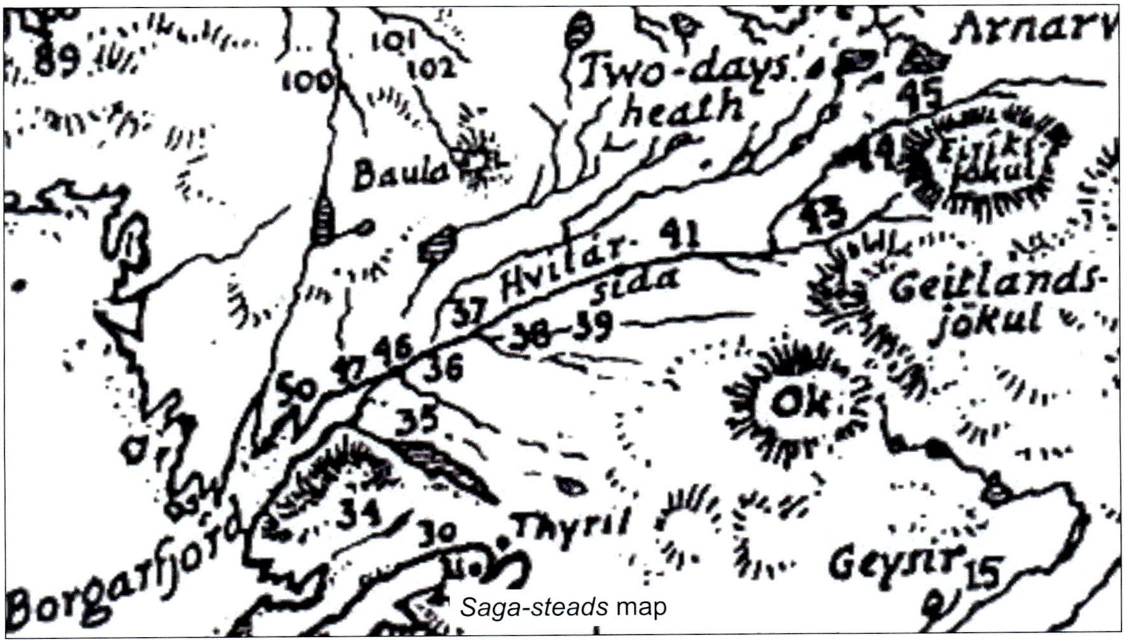

Saga-steads map

LETTERS FROM ICELAND No. 11

To: Robin Collingwood - aged 8.

Robin at Lanehead

Abbot Hall

Reykjavík. July 29. 1897.

Now Bobbin my boy, I'm to tell you how we took our longest day's ride - over 50 miles, and twelve hours in the saddle - with other exciting things.

Our guide was very late in coming and when he came it was quite afternoon. The Sysselman wanted Dr. Stefánsson and me to ride his horses; He came too, and the young farmer of Kornsá. So there were five men and ten horses in the company: and just as we started Peter told me to mind what I was doing, or that horse would run away with me. So I was rather frightened and held on tight. He did gallop a bit and jumped and so on: but nothing like the horse Dr. Stefánsson rode, who fairly bolted over the level grassy plain of the valley. We saw a man riding in the deepest part of the river and wondered if he was mad; but he said he was trying the depth for fishing: and indeed they catch fine trout and salmon and we often had some for supper, fresh caught and cooked with lots of butter. People eat butter and cream like anything; there is so much of them: and I've often drunk a quart of milk at a time. But most of the food isn't very nice.

Abbot Hall

'Sysselman Johannes Johannason'

As we started so late, it was evening when we got to the last farm before the mountains, and our guide wanted to stay there, which we didn't like, because it made us pay for a day more than we meant. However, we did: and made an excursion on his horses, - mine went capitally, - to a lonely valley where Grettir wrestled with Glam the ghost. It was an outlying farm, now a ruin: and Glam had been a thrall. In the winter he had died, and turned into a very wicked ghost, who rode the roof and killed the cows and frightened people. So one night when he came Grettir grabbed him and they had an awful fight, which ended in Grettir's smashing the ghost. I don't know how it all happened in reality, but the place is there, and I drew it. In the evening as I was drawing the sunset there came by a drove of 150 horses, going over our pass. They call such a drove a stoð; and four men and several dogs were with them to take them from the north of Iceland to the south. These horses are shipped to

Abbot Hall

'Blöndal, Stefánsson and Sysselman at Kornsá'

Abbot Hall
'Kornsá'

England to work in mines - which is rather a sad thing for them - to be always under ground, dragging trucks of coal, instead of galloping about on the moors in Iceland. But it was a curious sight to see so many at once coming up the path in that lonely place with only four men to guide them. Next day we saw the whole lot resting in a valley, after passing part of the desert. I said I'd like to photograph them but there was no sun - so they (the men and not the horses) said they would catch us up on the road and be taken. We went miles and miles over moors with mountains round in the distance - and towards evening came to a big lake full of fish - so that if you put in a bare hook they will bite at it. We met swans and cygnets everywhere, nesting in the moor, and our guide said that they catch the old swans when they are shedding their feathers and can't fly by riding after them and netting them: and the young ones by shouting at them, which so frightens them that they fall down and lie flat on the ground. Lots of ptarmigan we saw, and foxes: once a fox barked out of his hole, and frightened the horses. By the lake called Arnarvatn is a hut built for travellers to rest in. It was where we meant to sleep, but we found it kneedeep in mud, and though there was a spade put there to

Abbot Hall
Kornsá (18 July 1897)

Abbot Hall

'Thórhallsstadir', *Saga-steads* 141 (19 July 1897)

R.G. Collingwood Society

clean it out, I said I simply wouldn't: and so we rode on, thinking to get to Surtshellir a famous cave near Eriks[1]jökull, a great volcano extinct, and covered with snow and glaciers. Our guide Magnús Blöndal, rather wanted to take us to the top, which is not very difficult. An outlaw Eric once ran to the top to escape his enemies; but they chased him up, and killed him there, and so the place got its name. However, I didn't care for the long snow walk; and in the end, as it was getting night, and we had ridden 12 hours, not counting rests, we determined to camp out. Magnús was for sleeping on the grass; but I knew better, and picked myself a good place on a sandy spot under a big stone. We had smoked mutton and bread and whisky for supper; and I spread my holdall out, with the filled part for a pillow: tucked my feet under my saddle, and slept like a top: only waking when the 150 horses went by to camp out in the same place. Poor Magnús who slept on the grass, and Dr Stefánsson who did likewise, didn't sleep at all, but had a miserable night in the wet fog by the river, where the flies bit so that the horses ears were all over blood. In the morning the horsedrovers made coffee with a spirit lamp and gave us some. It was very funny and jolly, and they were as polite as if they were gentlemen inviting us to a party. Then we rode off through the fog, and through deep rivers, till we came to a queer grassy valley where the outlaws of the cave hid their horses and weapons when they went sheep stealing. At last the fog cleared, and it was a burning hot day, Eiriksjökull blazing in snow above, and wild lava fields all round. In this lavafield is Surtshellir, the great cave which nobody has ever come to the end of. We got into the outlaw's part of it, and saw their sleeping places, and the heaps of bones of the sheep they ate, and their fireplaces, and a cave of which the floor was all ice, - great rock halls, lit by holes in the roof, but dismal to live in. Then the others went away and left me to sketch. I was there for hours in the blazing sun, alone in the wilderness - miles and miles away from anybody. I got very tired and at last the <u>stoð</u> came by, and I took snapshots at them, to the great delight of the drovers, who gave me their address and asked for a copy of the photograph when it was developed: though I'm afraid it was hardly a good subject for a Kodak. After a long while Dr. Stefansson came back with a boy, from the nearest farm - a long way off - and candles to see the cave in another part. We each had a candle, and crept in over great rocks that cover the floor: and* then* found a hall of ice. Ice floor, and icicles all round, some standing up like pillars, and some hanging from the roof - and in one place a great curtain of icicles across the cave,

'Where they threw the sheep down'

Abbot Hall

'Árni Eiríksson and Stöð (140 ponies)'

Teresa Smith

Abbot Hall

'Streams coming out under the lava-field and over the rock, and falling into the Hvítá, below the bridge'

with a door through. It was rather pretty to see a light behind all the transparent and glittering lines and cones* and fringes, and organ pipes and railings and statues, and clear crystal drapes* of frost. But I confess the chief pleasure was to break off icicles and suck them, after such a roasting day: and I can't tell how much ice I ate. When we got out, we rode to the farm, Kalmanstunga, very prettily Alpine in situation: and found the stoð, and the drivers[2] eating curds at the farm. I had some too - and painted a portrait of a child, as well as the view - and then we rode fast in the evening through a pretty bushy valley - they call it forest, but none of the bushes are more than about 6 feet high - to Gilsbakki, a place where one of the saga people lived, on the hillside between two great gills. Snow mountains opposite and a great valley filled with ancient lava from Eiriksjökull. The lava is very curious, like curdled stuff in wrinkles and huge bubbles and cracks and cliffs - broken and tumbled about in the queerest and most fanciful way, and all the holes filled with flowers and little pretty plants: a sort of natural rock garden. But it is hardly paintable: it is curious rather than beautiful. The water that falls on the lava field (which is of course all cold and dead now) sinks through the cracks and comes out at the edge in springs and cascades, where you see the lava overlying the real rock: and along the cliffy riverbank there are innumerable falls as if the white butter were being squeezed out of the sandwich. At Gilsbakki we stayed with the clergyman and said goodbye to our guide: having got out of the North country into the South. And so another part of the journey was done.

I'm very glad you have been contributing to Nothing Much, and hope to see many nice things when I get home. Capital fun to play chess in bed, I should think. Perhaps you'll teach your Daddy.

---

1 W.G.C. writes 'Erics' with a 'c' here.

2 'Dr*i*vers' - otherwise he has written 'drovers'.

LETTERS FROM ICELAND No. 12

To: Ursula Collingwood - aged 6.

Reykjavík. July 29. 1897

Dearest Ursula,

This fifth and last sheet of my story is for you - in return for your nice little letter.

'Ursula Mavis' by E.M.D.Collingwood

Abbot Hall

I told Robin how we got to Gilsbakki, and about the lavafield. Now next day, the clergyman took us through it and over a bridge which they're very proud of: because bridges are great rarities in Iceland. Our horses are extremely frightened of bridges; and very unhappy when they come to made roads. They are accustomed to mountain paths, and they think bridges are a sort of trap to bite them. We took them over very carefully, and then saw a splendid waterfall called Barnafoss, the barn's force, because there used to be a rock bridge over it, as at Dungeon Gill, and some children tried to cross it, and fell in and were killed. The rainbow in the fall was beautiful and such rocks and foam! Then the clergyman left us and before long we lost the way and wandered on a moor but in the end got to Reykholt, where a great writer used to live, named Snorri Sturluson. He had a house on a hill, at the foot of which are several hot springs, which bubble up and steam away right out of the ground. He built a round bath with seats made so that you could sit up to your neck in hot water, and arranged watercourses so that hot or cold could be put in, because the water is <u>boiling</u>, and the people <u>cook</u> in it: baked bread for us that very evening, by putting a pan of dough in the spring. In Snorri's time the bath was covered over, but now the building has fallen down, but the bath is there, and Dr. Stefánsson had a hot bath next morning while I drew the place.

In the river below is another spring of boiling water, coming out of a rock that stands up over the flat river bed - so that there is hot and cold at once. We rode into the river and got our horses up to the place - though they didn't like it at all: and we climbed on to

Abbot Hall

'Barnafoss'

Abbot Hall

'Barnafoss Bridge'

the rock which was quite hot and shaky with the fizzling hot fountain. Finally we turned up at a farm called Deildartunga near a whole family of hot springs that stream and steam out of a red rock by the river. At Deildartunga we met a man called Sveinn* Oddson who was going our way, a nice man, with a little boy on a horse to himself, travelling back after bringing his wife and baby to Deildartunga to stay. The little boy rode capitally and only was annoyed because his father took away the whip he was using too much. We rode with them for a good while through a rather dull part, chiefly stones and sand and rivers, till the mountains of Skorradale began to look very big and near. One, the Skessuhorn, is rather like a small Matterhorn - not so very small neither: and close to these craggy and snowy mountains is a lake, with one side low hills and the other side high ones, like Coniston. Just about where Lanehead would be is a farm called Grund, and there we stayed the night, sleeping in a tiny bedroom which got very stuffy before morning and the window wouldn't open. The next day was wet and we rode sulkily down the river, away from Reykjavík where I wanted to get letters, towards Borg, which was a place we were obliged to see because Egil Skallagrimson lived there: also we had been told a steamer called there on the 26th that could take us straight to Reykjavík. I was hoping this would be our last ride on that journey, as we had too much luggage for the horses, and they were tired, and we were dirty, and wanted clean clothes and a rest. At Hvitarvellir, where the farmer has been in England, and keeps a very big place in fine style, we stayed first to dinner; then, waiting for the rain to stop, to supper and bed. Next day I found that my horse had a swelling on his back: and the son of the farmer offered to take him at rather less than half what he cost me, and to sell me another - which I was forced to do, for he could not be ridden. So late in the day we got off, and stopped at several places to draw, and at last got to Borg, at the

Abbot Hall

'Reykholt, Snorralaug' 23 July 1897

head of a bay one side of which is Borgarness, where the steamers call. And there was the steamer, far in the distance. We couldn't believe it: but the clergyman said it had already whistled to start - and he sent a man to ride galloping round and stop it if possible. Before the man had gone far the steamer was off and away, and there we were miles and miles from Reykjavík. I proposed hiring a sailboat, but everybody was too busy - with haymaking. I was rather disappointed and cross - but there was no help for it and we had to ride three days round to get where 5 hours by steamboat would have brought us, if we had only been half an hour sooner at the place. It turned out that the steamer did indeed call the next day, but outward bound, and nobody had the sense to explain that.

However I made a lot of sketches, and Síra Einar the clergyman gave me various presents, of old locks and bits of metal work and promised to send a fine wooden crucifix (from the pre-Reformation time) to Reykjavík for me. He was extremely kind - a nice handsome brighteyed man - and rode with us next day to Borgarness to see Skallagrim's grave and so forth: and so we came back to Hvitarvellir and Grund for the night.

I forgot to say that Hvitarvellir is a place where they ferry you over the river, and the horses swim behind the boat. Coming back the new horse, who had done it often before took the water easily, but the old horse, who had done it once only and didn't like it, was very troublesome. I had to get out of the boat, and thrash him well before he would go in: but when he got in he swam like a duck, and they both got over capitally - and then the boat came back for me.

Abbot Hall

'Krummskelda - Skallagrim's bog' 25 July 1897

Abbot Hall

'Gufáróss', *Saga-steads* 47 25 July 1897

R.G. Collingwood Society

At Grund everybody was in bed when we arrived but they got up and put us in our old quarters - though we only had milk for supper. Next day we went by the lake and over 2 passes to Hvalfjördr, where we got a man and a boat - and another man to take the horses round the head of the fjord while we rowed to Geirsholmi, a steep island on which outlaws once lived. We went up the rock - it was real ladderclimbing, and there is only one place where it is possible, and disturbed the puffins from their nests. The outlaws must have had a bad time there - cold and exposed. In the end they were invited on shore, on pretence of making peace - and all massacred: only Helga the wife of the chief and an Earl's daughter swam away to land with her two babies, and carried them up the hill and saved them. We had a dreadful hard row to get to the other side against a storm that had sprung up, and a wet dismal ride over a high pass and down a terrible, awful zigzag track to Reynivellir. There the people were building a new house and had just pulled down part of the old one to use the wood. The clergyman's wife (he was away) let us sleep in the church, which is against the law - but there we slept - I inside the altar rails, like in a cot: but I slept all the same.

(End) The last day, yesterday, was very wet and stormy. We had a long and miserable ride over a pass, and by long wet roads to this place. And so ends the story of our big journey -

Ever your loving daddy - W.G.C.

The Collingwood Altarpiece at Borg Church

W.G. Collingwood visited Borg on 25/26 July 1897 and stayed with the pastor, Einar Friðgeirsson (see Letter No. 12). When they reached Reykjavík he wrote a letter of thanks [Reykjavík, National Library of Iceland, Lbs 3175a 4to]:

August 13 1897
Hotel Reykjavík, Reykjavík

Dear Sir,

We came back from our travels last night, and got your kind present today. I am very much obliged, and thank you heartily for it, and for all your goodness, which I shall not forget. We had a long ride to the south, Fljótshlíð and Skálholt, Geysir and Thingvellir; and, as I feared, our horses were tired, and their backs were sore, especially the strong cream-coloured pony's. We did not feel that it could travel farther, and left both at Thingvellir. If we could have brought them back in good condition we might have taken advantage of your kind offer; but they were not good enough to send you, in that damaged state.

When I get home I will see about the picture for your church, and you shall have the best that can be done.

With compliments to your wife and kind remembrances to the children, I am always yours faithfully

W.G. Collingwood

In July 2012, the modern Collingwood Icelandic Pilgrimage visited Borg church. The photograph shows Teresa Smith and the present pastor Þorbjörn Hlynur Árnarson by the altarpiece painted by her grandfather. Collingwood used his own children as models for the children in the painting, including Teresa's father Robin.

Mike Lea

Excerpts from W.G. Collingwood's diary

1897

23 September. Worked at Borg altarpiece.
24 September. Worked at Borg picture.
25 September. Borg pict.
27 September. Painted from Robin & Ursula on Borg altarpiece.
28 September. Painted from Dora, Borg picture.
29 September. Borg picture.
30 September. Borg picture.
1 October. Borg picture.
2 October. Borg picture.

1898

10 June. Painted at Borg altarpiece all day.
12 June. Wrote to Síra Einar Friðgeirsson at Borg that I hoped the altarpiece wd reach him in the course of next month.
20 June. Mr Lund sat for St Peter in the altarpiece.
29 June. Borg altarpiece.
1-6 July (bracketed together). Borg altarpiece – hammer and tongs.
6 July. Completed painting in of the Borg picture.
7 July. Borg picture.
11 July. Packed altarpiece & sent it, with letter to Einar Friðgeirsson.

Þjóðminjasafn Íslands, Ívar Brynjólfsson

'Christ Blessing the Little Children'

Reykjavík

28 - 30 July 1897

LETTERS FROM ICELAND No. 13

To: Mrs. Collingwood

Hotel Reykjavík, Reykjavík, Iceland.

P.S.
<u>See back of this</u>

July 29, 1897
Eight o'clock evening.

We came to this hotel because Hotel Island was full. We had a little stuffy room last night - but people are moving off by the Laura tonight and we are put into bigger and better rooms.

I want a day or 2 to overhaul sketches - many people want to see them - some want an Exhn. and M. P's (Althing now sitting) to be invited. Dr. Jón has raised £10. - from Jón Magnússon[1] the governor's secretary, his friend (and Eirik Magnússon's enemy!). That means we can do the rest of our task - with economy: and I believe it is really worth while both for my own sake - and for the sake of the people who are interested in the undertaking. I don't set much store on promises - but there is evidently a strong feeling that our book, being the only thing of its kind, will meet the very great desire of Icelanders here and in America to see their sagas and country illustrated. And if I only half do it, it will cause disappointment.

So I hope you will balance whatever little disappointment may be caused by the delay against the greater disappointment of failure in the work - and as the loan is so freely given I take it that I must accept, and make use of it. Don't mind a few days more. I was to come by the boat that will bring you this on the 6th[2] - now we go to Thingvaller, Geysir, Hliðarendi (Gunnar's Lithend[3]) and that part - returning in 10 days to catch the Thyra on the 14th - which goes round Iceland - into all the fjords, and reaches Leith 28th Aug.

Can you send a cheque for £25. on Aug. 11th[4] to
the Rev H. A. Starkie
Townhead
Pendleton
Clitheroe, Lancashire

and if not, write to him and say I'm away - and back on the 29th and asking him to wait. But I suppose you can -

If my father is with you give my love, and tell him the news; if not please write him a line - I've been all day writing to Lanehead - and a note to Ellwood.

~~If you write to me Hotel Reykjavik~~
~~Reykjavik~~
~~Iceland~~
~~and post on the 29th August it will reach on the~~

No - this [is] a mistake. You can't answer this - except by a line to Leith - to me,

Poste Restante
Leith N.B.

for me to get there on arriving on the 28th Aug - I will then telegraph to you - and I hope and pray to get back then, and with my work done - I must shut up now to post by Laura -

Your loving W.G.C.

Note: This half sheet to Mrs. Collingwood, might count as the second page of letter No 8. - but it is so clearly written after the four letters to the children that I have treated it as a letter in its own right. (It was written at speed, and is not entirely legible.)

1 Jón Magnússon (1859-1926) Governor's Secretary 1896-1904.
2 The 6th August, the day he had hoped to arrive home, was his birthday.
3 'Lithend' - elsewhere, and in the *Saga-steads*, he writes this 'Lythend' (familiar to us in 'Lyth Valley').
4 'cheque for £25 ...' the quarter's rent for Lanehead.

LETTERS FROM ICELAND No. 14

To: Mrs. Collingwood

Hotel Reykjavík.
Reykjavík
Iceland
July 30. 1897

Darlingest Molly,

Your letter of the 18th of June came today - sent, I suppose, from the other hotel where it had been overlooked. I thought there was something wanting - but I didn't know how to get at it - as we applied twice to the people there, and had all the poste restante letters searched at the post office. However the Vesta sails on the 3rd. and you'll get this not so long after the letters sent in the Laura - 2 days, I think. Then no more until I write by a boat, the Botnia, going the 15th. which will bring you letters on the 22nd, and we hope to reach Leith on the 28th. by the Thyra starting 14th. but going north and all round Iceland first.

This plan will let us visit and sketch all the important places. I feel wicked at being longer than my time - but it's for a good purpose!

People who have seen the sketches today express great interest - and wonder how I got so much done. It is wet; and the storm (which makes me not sorry to be ashore) seems to be spending itself. Tomorrow we hope to start south east to the great plains under the snow mountains of Hekla and Eyjafell, to see the sites of Njál's Saga, and then turning north to the Geyser, and west to Thingvaller,[1] to return by the 12th. ready to catch the Thyra. We shall have next to no luggage this trip, and much more experience in travelling, so I hope things will go more easily. This hotel is more English than the other, though smaller. One gets food that one recognises as food - and last night I slept in a comfortable spring bed - not between two eiderdown pillows with toes out. The rest is pleasant, and I have spent the day in overhauling and showing sketches. One of our friends here wanted to know if it was I who wrote the Life of Ruskin - which he had found about in the <u>Conversations* Lexicon</u> - a German Encyclopaedia. But I think Dr. Jón finds me rather difficult to drag out into the society of Reykjavík: and indeed after weeks of hard work one feels what Ursula calls in some glum state, and not inclined to cheapen one's affability: - more to smoke in one's bedroom. But I have to go about a little.

If I'd time I'd like to gossip about the people: but they all run into types - English old maids globe trotting - fishermen with rods broken and no salmon - Germans gobbling (but not more than I) and so forth, beside the Icelanders and their politics. Magnús Magnússon[2] is here, very bored, and with little prospect of doing anything: and his uncle is the bête noire of the officials.

My guide philosopher and friend comes and wants me to go out in the wet to see people - bother!

Evening. 11 o'clock. We went to get my watch which had stopped weeks ago - and there's nobody to mend it except here. The spring had broken, the úrsmiðr said, and charged 4½ kroner. Anyhow it is ticking merrily again. Then to the College to see Herr Doctor Rector Björn Olsen, who proposed to ride with us tomorrow morning, as he is starting for his holiday. Then to the Lector - head of Theological College and Speaker of the Parliament now sitting, Síra Thorhallur Bjárnarson - father of the funny little Dora. He was not back from the Althing - but his wife entertained us - and another lady who was calling. They talked Icelandic to me and I replied in English: with occasional help on both sides from Dr Jón. So we passed an hour, and conversation flagged and we started to go, but saw that - how can I escape tautology? - the flag was down which showed that the sitting was ended - and soon the speaker came in breathless - for he had expected us. He kindly fell in with Stefánsson's plan of getting a grant from Parliament for our book: a plan which (as you would guess) does not meet my ideas; and I tried to explain why: though it seems that very little encouragement would do it, as the book to illustrate Iceland is quite - what shall I say? - the talk of the town. I declined to show specimen drawings to a committee, & refused a subsidy: I've lots of good reasons: and then we had rum syllabub and walked home in the dark - for it is night now - so long after midsummer. I think Dr. Jón thinks me a troublesome person: but I can't show half done sketches or modify my plans, and I haven't time to finish sketches for exhibition here, though I show them to private friends. And it isn't for me to take the money of poor little Iceland, who can't afford - anything of the necessaries of civilisation. If an English publisher takes the book, he will do the job: if not, the Iceland government can't do more than a bit of it.

I'm glad you like the Coniston book[3] - and that the children ride well. I'm not going to bring a pony home so don't be afraid[4]. And I'm glad to have all your dear letters now.

Saty. 31st. half past ten. Weather improving - horses saddled - had a good English breakfast, and just starting - much love to you all - send word to Bristol please.

(This letter does not carry any signature.)

1 'Thingvaller' is what W.G.C. wrote here.

2 Magnús Magnússon (1873-1965) brother and foster-son of Eiríkr Magnússon (1833-1913).

3 *The Book of Coniston* (1897) had just been printed.

4 In 1871 William Morris had shipped his pony, Mouse, home to Kelmscott.

Njáls saga country and Þingvellir

31 July to 14 August 1897

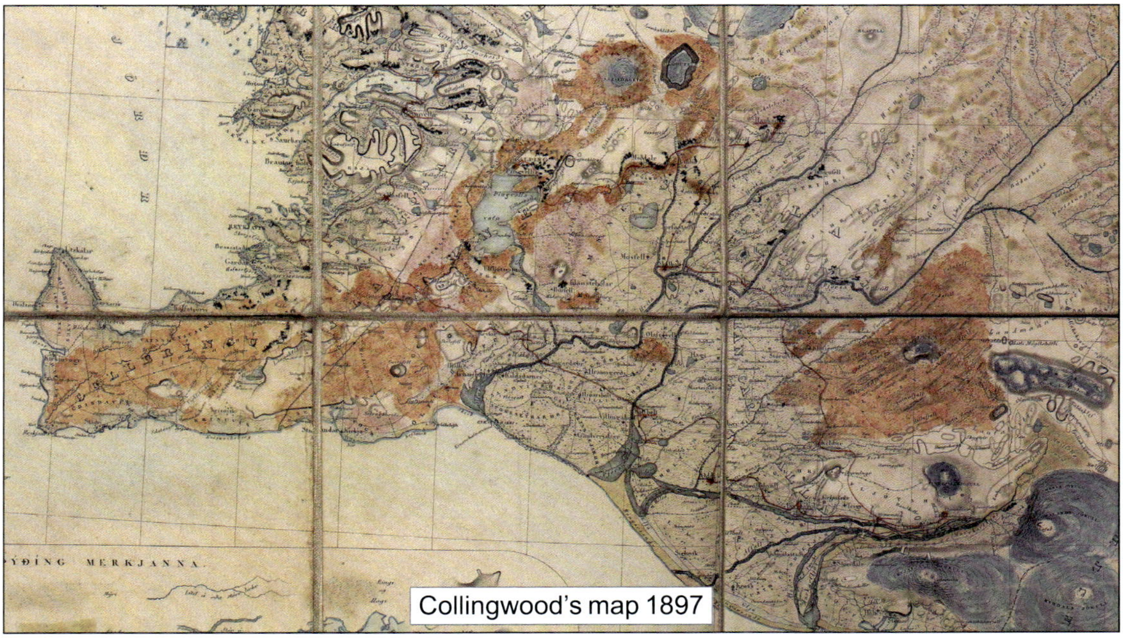

Collingwood's map 1897

Saga-steads map

LETTERS FROM ICELAND No. 15

To: Mrs. Collingwood

Hotel Reykjavík.
Aug 13. Friday. half past
six in the morning.

Darlingest Molly,

I am glad and sorry to be at the end of the two months ride - and glad without sorry that we get on board today for the voyage back to home and you. We go by the Thyra reaching Leith Aug 28 - this letter goes by Botnia, reaching Leith Aug 21 - and I hope you'll get it on the 22nd. Then you will have nearly a week to write me an answer to Leith - Poste Restante - and I will call for this letter and telegraph to you on arrival. If you write on the 27th - or say the 26th in case we should happen to be a day before our time as the Laura was in coming here - then I shall get news in a fortnight from now. And in writing tell me whether you'd like me to come back in a beard, or whether I must cut it off before appearing instead of after:[1] and please send me ten pounds - not in a cheque: but either in notes or order - perhaps Miss Bownass[2] will tell you what is the best way to Poste Restante. The post is not far from the boat, but I think it is better to address like that than to address to the Steamer: for I shall be eager to get ashore, and might miss whatever budget of letters comes aboard. The money I want, to pay back Dr. Stefánsson and to get my ticket home. He is going to Denmark, I think; - and I think £10 will clear me: if not I must send the money to him afterwards.

When I wrote last we were starting for the South. Of course we made a later start than we intended, & did not get off in time to travel with Dr. Björn Olsen. Instead, we picked up with a ruffianly looking farmer, a sort of Tom Seagrim - black haired and unshaved for a fortnight; riding miserable looking horses and leading a little girl bundled up on the top of a side saddle. He turned out to be a very nice fellow, and the little girl, three years old, one of the pluckiest of travellers. It came on wetter and wetter, and when we got to the halfway house on Hellisheiði it poured. The place was crowded with an excursion from Reykjavík - young - what wd. be called 'gentlemen' in England: all kicking up a great row - and drunk. The Editor of Sunnanfari, an Icelandic magazine published in Copenhagen was particularly incoherent and absurd. They don't mind these things here: except when English sailors make a row in the drinking houses at Reykjavík. The English bear the blame of many things and the Icelander keeps a good conceit of himself. - However we saw the beggars all ride off - and they can stick on their horses however screwed they are (- except that half the deaths seem to be from that combination of whisky and water which is made by fording rivers when they are drunk -).

Then we got food and drink and started in the driving downpour across the Hellisheiði which is a high moorland of lava, with hot springs now and then and extinct volcanic places - loathsome, and yet in the thick mist and rain so veiled as to be mysterious and interesting. It was a dismal long ride until we got to a zigzag - for this was a made road, lately opened, one of 2 such wheel roads in the country - and the cloud thinned and parted and we saw the plain of the south unrolled before us in the twilight, with the sea beyond: and black precipitous ranges blocking the landward side; and cloud ceiling very thick and dreary. It rained still: and by nightfall we began to press the farmer to leave his little girl at a farm instead of going ten miles farther with a very tired child, but she said she would rather go on. We plunged thro' kneedeep mud*3 along a tröd to a baer, and got her milk: and then away through a river in the twilight - the youngster wagging like a doll tied on a dog - but so wrapped that she couldn't fall or get cold. The farmer showed us the place where we could stay, and rode into the dark with his little girl. We had ridden about 40 miles - she had to ride about 50: but then she was going home. Her home had been tumbled down by the earthquakes in the autumn, and she had been taken to Reykjavík for the winter, until they could build a new house. So that was why the bóndi looked a raggamuffin - poor chap.

Kortstrand was a clean new farm, rebuilt after earthquakes, and a regular traveller's house of call. We were wet through - heads arms and legs - and next morning put on wet clothes again. They said the Kitchen leaked, since the earthquakes, and so they couldn't dry the clothes. I didn't see the argument - and merely felt that wherever Icelanders are in the habit of seeing many travellers they get corrupted very rapidly. They are hospitable in remote parts from curiosity and simplicity. But they soon lose the liking for guests and take the silly attitude of '<u>We</u> don't ask them to come; they needn't come and if they don't like it' - all the while pocketing twice, or more than twice what is good pay in the west and north. And I find that no Icelander tells the plain truth - partly from an Irish wish to please; but more from a certain muddleheadedness, and entire absence of definite training to observe and deal with facts. If they are at all clever they are literary - lots of poets as they are called in a land where all geese are swans. But nobody seems to have any idea of the scientific fact, or the business facts, or the political fact - or any other fact. It's all what they fancy.

So we hated Kortstrand, and went off cross. The horses were cross too after a wet night in which they must have got no rest. Mine lay down in the mud, with me on his back, and began to roll himself: and we went on most wretchedly to the suspension bridge over the Olfusá - a thing the Icelanders are furiously proud of - and still along the good new road over level ground - all marsh with holts or bits of stony hills standing up like islands - and every holt has a farm - and the marsh between serves as pastureland. At last a family came along, gentleman and lady and little girl evidently of the better class. It was Sunday, but I thought it must be a parson, and so he turned out to be, a Síra Ofeigr, travelling from Reykjavík. We rode a good bit with him - and his little girl too rode capitally and sat up like a little trooper. The lady seemed to be not her mother but somebody who was being taken to the country. They went to a farm off the road to get a meal - and we floundered on through a part where the road is still being made; the old road destroyed and the new one all mud and cobble stones. It was frightful work, and our horses wouldn't go or would go wrong. At last we led them over a moor where there was scarcely any track or guide except the tops of the suspension bridge (No. 2) over the next big river. I didn't draw that either: which all good Icelanders will regret. The parson and party had caught us up at the bridge, and he tried to direct Dr. J.S. who misunderstood - and an hour

Abbot Hall

'Kálfholt - house of Síra Ólafur Finnsson'

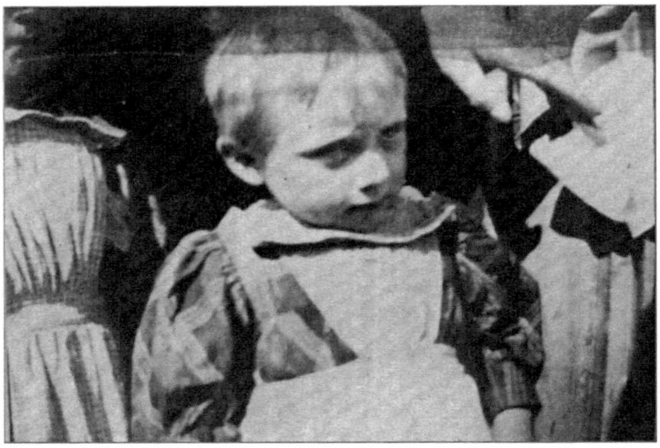

Abbot Hall

Abbot Hall

'Children of Síra Ólafur Finnsson'

after we were again caught up by Síra Ofeigr, and this time taken into the right 'road' (in English 'sheep-track') for our next harbourage Kálfholt.

There we were received by a very handsome girl with whom I was rapidly falling in love, when in the middle of conversation she turned her head and hawked and spat, and then went on talking. She was the clergyman's wife's sister (as usual at parsonages - there's always a young sister.) Síra Olafur was away. Parsons have to ride to their 'chapels of ease' for very long journeys - many hours over the worst roads, to preach to a handful of unsympathetic parishioners, taking a service at each church once a month or less often - and then to ride home as well as they can. Some have to go thirty or forty miles out and the same back: and nobody cares a hang for the sermon when its preached. In Kálfholt the grave stones of the former parsons were made into steps for the church door, broken and defaced. I dragged one out and photographed it; they have a quaint triptych altarpiece which of course they want to get rid of, for a modern Danish picture in the style of the chromo lithograph of our nurseries thirty years ago. But we saw worse things afterwards. I had a bedroom to myself - a sort of closet hall filled with the parson's dogeared books and various rubbish - (every room is a wardrobe and storeroom in Iceland) and we had good food and kindness from the people - the wife was nice and Síra Olafur not a bad chap at all. 2 children, one pretty. Regular travellers place, Dr. Kahle had been there; but most ungetatable, with no road or path to it from any side - bogs all round - utterly unimaginable to the English mind of the present age.

Abbot Hall

'Altar of Kálfholt Church'

We started with a boy to show us through the bogs (and to do a bit of business for the parson) and found that we had been taken far out of our way, when we got to Sandholaferja* - Sandhillferry - down the river - not far from the sea. So we got another guide, a young man who is going to Edinburgh infirmary for an operation - but nevertheless rode all the day with us over mires, and by a big bleak tarn, and up a river valley - in which the 'road' is economically managed by taking the sandy river shore - and as this appears and reappears alternately on this side and that - you simply cross the river to get to it. Sometimes the river can't be crossed: and then the road doesn't exist. People don't. The rain had swollen the water a little; one had to tuck feet up behind the saddle: and we crossed, our guide said, 18 times. It must have been 17 or 19 for we left off on the opposite side rather tired of the Rauðalaekr - Rothayleck. It is great fun to see the little collie dogs of the country, who always come these trips, swimming the fords, and carried far down and then racing up the banks. This time the creature knew we should recross the water, and saved himself many a swim. After the final farewell to Rauðalaekr our guide left us, with advice to call at Ægisiða to be helped over the Rangá which was a bad ford. So when we came to a big farm by a big river we turned in and took coffee and the farmer saddled his horse and showed us over the ford. It was wide and deep and a strong current, but my pipe didn't go out in crossing it, and I didn't get a drop of wet except the tips of my boot toes. Then we turned south over sandy plains and grass and more mire to Oddi.

We saw Oddi in the distance rising like a big artificial barrow in the plain, with the tops of houses appearing over the ridge of the hill, and we got there before sunset, riding through the hay to the big new house - big as they make them here and new with corrugated iron roof. Síra Skuli is very proud of it, and rather objected to the view I chose because this new house would be partly hidden by the ugly old turf farm - they always call a timberhús fine, and a turfhouse ljótr - ugly. Síra Skuli is one of the richest parsons in the South and has a very big farm: a wife from Reykjavík, and children who do what they are told and don't paw my sketches - quite unique in Iceland where children are often pretty, but usually spoiled and bad mannered. I got a sketch of Oddi in the sunset - it was very damp, but a fine effect. And next morning - Oh, I get on too fast. We slept in a tiny bedroom, in 2 beds, which left only another bed's space between them, and that was filthy with candle droppings (which must have been left since winter or spring) and rubbish and dust, the leg of a doll, bits of paper, and a battered filthy old skin of I don't remember what animal. This opened out of a rather grand drawing room: and the window didn't open. Consequently the room was very foul in the morning, and not to be ventilated except into the drawing room. This is one of the best houses in the South, and the mistress a Reykjavík lady - very nice and pleasant all the same. Of course nights spent in such rooms are no refreshment: even the morning coffee does not clear one's head, and the crossness deepens through the day with the folly and the filth of this land of boors. I sketched one of the children at Oddi, and a view from the churchyard, where Saemund is buried. He was the great bishop who wrote the older Edda - i.e. the book of Oddi and they tell tales about him - and how the devil put dirt on the church door and Saemund commanded him to lick it off, and he licked so hard that he licked a hole in the stone, which remained until lately when Síra Matthias Jochumssen, the Unitarian and poet, being parson at Oddi, removed the stone, and put down instead a very fine grave stone, which is now obliterated as well as desecrated. Síra Skuli had sold the pulpit, which had old paintings of angels and devils: and now they have a joiner's contraption instead. At Breiðabolstaðr[4] - the next place we went to - the Governor, Magnus Stephensen, has taken a fine copper font bowl (with leave of the bishop) and given the church a common tin washhandbasin instead. The bishop doesn't think the chalice and paten there worth taking: they are early 14th century French silver gilt and enamelled things. I'm going to try to get them before the bishop hears of what I said. Evidently not a soul cares: and all they want is to get rid of every scrap of antiquity out of their churches. At this same place the parson is building him an house - and I saw the builder shoving into the stone walling which forms the foundation, scraps of tombstones: one bit had the date 1616. All these old stones

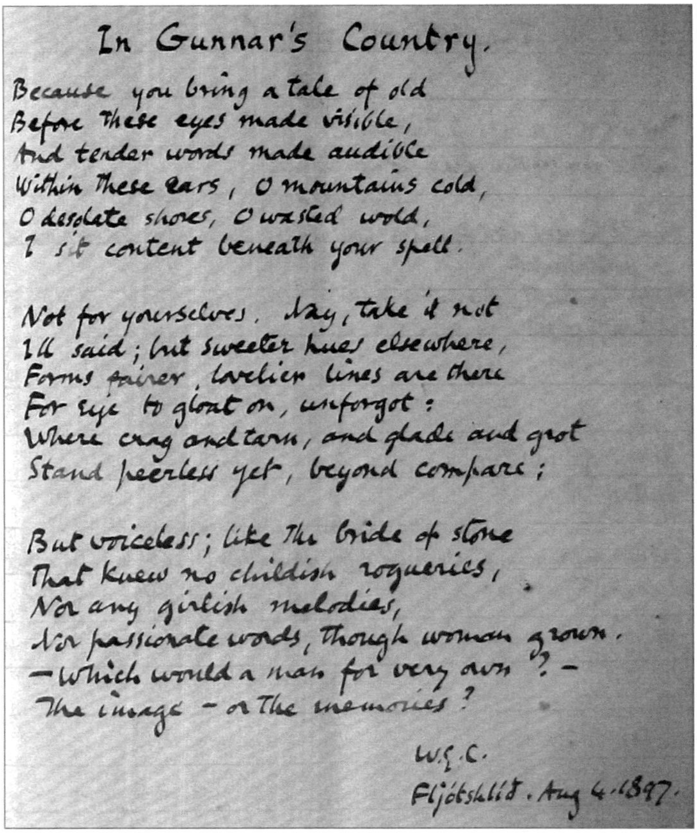
In Gunnar's Country.

Because you bring a tale of old
Before these eyes made visible,
And tender words made audible
Within these ears, O mountains cold,
O desolate shores, O wasted wold,
I sit content beneath your spell.

Not for yourselves. Nay, take it not
Ill said; but sweeter hues elsewhere,
Forms fairer, lovelier lines are there
For eye to gloat on, unforgot:
Where crag and tarn, and glade and grot
Stand peerless yet, beyond compare;

But voiceless; like the bride of stone
That knew no childish rogueries,
Nor any girlish melodies,
Nor passionate words, though woman grown.
— Which would a man for very own? —
The image — or the memories?

W.G.C.
Fljótshlíð. Aug 4. 1897.

Abbot Hall

'In Gunnar's Country' - in *Nothing Much*: Sept. 1897

are most decoratively carved, and wd. be splendid ornaments for any church: but they break them up and do anything with them rather than preserve them. The Breiðabolstaðr parson, Síra Eggerts gave us good skýr, and took us along Fljotshlið - i.e. the Lyth of the Fleet - the long hillside of this great spreading river - of which the Lyth End is Hliðarendi - Gunnar's home. We were to have gone farther, but I wanted to sleep at Hliðarendi, and we knocked the people up, and got a shakedown on the floor and a drink of milk in a poor and rough cottage where the famous hero once had his hall. I daresay you remember how they attacked him 40 to one, and how he defended himself till his bowstring was cut; and his wife would not give him 2 locks of her hair to make another - and how they pulled the roof off his house and finally killed him: and how he was seen singing in his howe one moonlight night - all these things everyone knows - and the house and the howe I have painted. Also how he was outlawed and was actually going abroad - but in crossing the river his horse stumbled and he stopped for a moment and looking back, saw his home, and said 'I mean to turn back; I will not go': and so went back to his death. I have crossed the river, and seen the view he saw and drawn it too.

But the place is changed. The river has burst through the plain where his fields were, so that now the farmer has to take his milkmaids twice a day over deep waters to milk the cows - and the next farm is now in the act of being moved - because its very site is being swept away by the water. We saw the banks caving in and turf lying in the river bed; the hay is being swept away before they can dry it & lead it, so fast the ravage is going on: and the whole great plain is a tangle of watercourses and a litter of stones.

The Lyth is pretty, with gill after gill, force after force, and farms nestling between, under the rocks, among green slopes of hay grass: and opposite rises Eyjafjallajökull, the Mont Blanc of these parts, with glaciers running down into the valley and crags above them, and snow dome in the clouds. Up the valley is Thorsmörk, the curiosity of the place. I wanted to draw the glaciers, and so Dr. J.S. went to Thorsmörk in the evening, slept in a cave among ferns and moss and flowers - rocks and glaciers, and every thing that the land

Abbot Hall

'Skemma at Hliðarendi'

Teresa Smith

'Bær of Hliðarendi'

contains in epitome*. He got back midday afterwards, and we were starting but it came on to rain, and rained harder and harder. So we stayed at Barkarstaðir another night, though I didn't like the stink of my bed and the food was very badly cooked - awfully badly. They killed a lamb for us, and served up chunks of burnt and bleeding flesh. The first night when I was alone - after travelling and drawing all day - what do you think I got for supper? A plate of thin rice pudding with sultanas in it. It was taken away and I hoped for something substantial: but the next course came on - another plate of thin rice pudding with sultanas in it. This I managed to put down - and hoped for something substantial when Tómas the bóndi (exactly like Raven the tailor[5]) stalked in, round the room, approached closer and closer, looked me earnestly in the eyes and 'will you a coffee?' said he. 'Ju, tak' said I; and got coffee and cakes. The wife really had meant to make me a feast by her cookery: but I'd rather have had bread and butter.

The next day was melancholy because it was the 6th of August[6] and the day I should have been home, seeing my Molly and all my little people, and how they looked and how much they'd grown. The whimbrel always shouts 'you dear, you dear' - so I can't forget them: but I've been too long away. It was wet - and we rode back to Hliðarendi and the farmer was glad to see us; had got himself up in his best Sunday clothes, and his best room was swept and garnished with black sand strewed in whirls, and there was skyr and coffee and tobacco and schnapps - and the fat little Gunnar much in evidence - for they are proud of owning the historic site: - and we had tipped handsome.

Abbot Hall

'Gunnar of Hliðarendi'

He took us over the Thrihyrning pass from which I saw Hekla with a rainbow over it in the distance - good subject, down to Reynifell: and soon after went back to pilot his milkmaids over Markarfljot after kissing us both very brotherly. Thence we went over lava to Keldur, where I read an indecipherable inscription and made a sketch - both of which impressed the people: and the farmer rode with us to Fellsmuli at least 20 miles over lava along the side of Hekla. We arrived very late, quite in the dark; but he insisted on returning. I can't imagine how

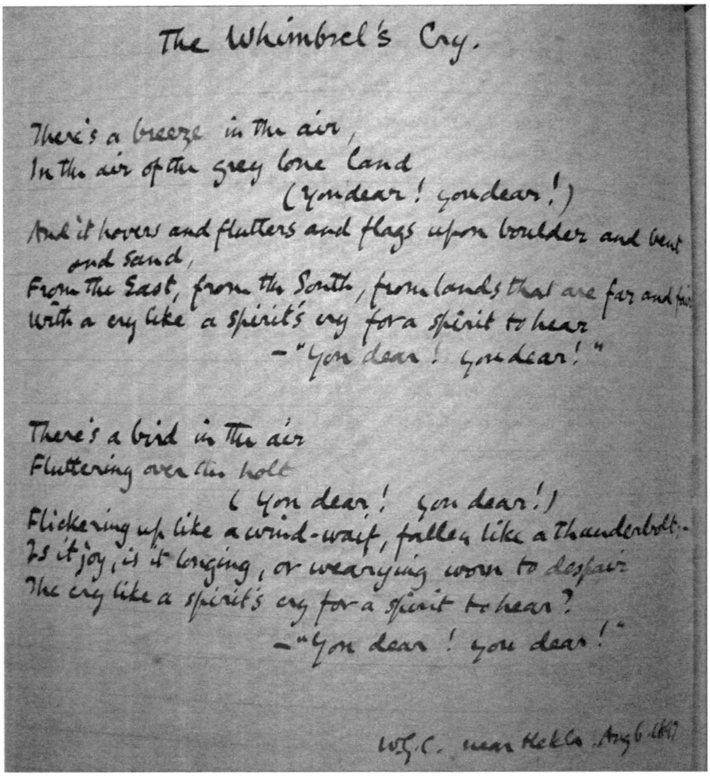

The Whimbrel's Cry.

There's a breeze in the air,
In the air of the grey lone land
(You dear! you dear!)
And it hovers and flutters and flags upon boulder and bent
and sand,
From the East, from the South, from lands that are far and fair
With a cry like a spirit's cry for a spirit to hear
— "You dear! you dear!"

There's a bird in the air
Fluttering over the holt
(You dear! you dear!)
Flickering up like a wind-waif, fallen like a thunderbolt,
Is it joy, is it longing, or wearying worn to despair
The cry like a spirit's cry for a spirit to hear?
— "You dear! you dear!"

W.G.C. near Hekla, Aug 6 1897

Abbot Hall

'The Whimbrel's Cry' - in *Nothing Much*: Sept 1897

he or his horses knew the way in the dark, but of course we do much the same thing on the water at home.

Fellsmuli is a poor little parsonage. I had the bedroom and Dr. J. S. the bed on the floor. Homoeopathic Doctor was there when we arrived, for a child with whoopingcough: very prevalent. Doctor went off into the night and left us in possession of the supper table and a lamp which 'has never gone right since the earthquakes.' I suggested more oil. The earthquakes are the great event and fact here. The house was thrown down, people had to sleep in haystacks. Only the mild weather prevented great loss of life from exposure. There are great cracks in the ground - which they are evidently proud of: for they prefer laming their horses in them to filling them up: interesting, of course: Korah, Dathan and Abiram business,[7] only nobody was bad enough to get nipped.

Síra Einar took us to the ferry of Thjörsá - where the water is deep and billowy - very difficult for the horses to swim, they refused to be driven and had to be led behind the boat. At the farm we got to know a little Barbara sort of girl who reads, Viktoria, her name is: evidently a clever child: and the farmer took us to the next place - broad calm ferry of Hvitá. Thence in the twilight through marshes to Skálholt - formerly cathedral, now huts and hovels round a miserable little chapel, under the floor of which lie the fine marble monuments of famous bishops, and ancient tombstones broken and scattered. The neighbourhood is all miry - a good reason for moving the bishop's see* - and we had a long weary ride through mud and water and rain to the geyser. It had spouted finely the evening before; 15 miles away it was a column of smoke against the blue mountains, visibly enormous. But when we were a mile away ...

<u>Evening</u>. Here I had to stop for getting up and breakfast - afterwards Síra Thorhallur, the speaker, and his wife, Síra Sigurður Gunnarsson of Stykkisholm, chairman of the Finance Committee and Arni Thorsteinsson,* the president of the Upper House, came to see the sketches - also Magnús Magnússon who is now settled, for the Althing has passed a vote giving him 2000 kroner a year as public teacher of gymnastics. Then I packed, and packed beautifully, with Magnus advising: then dinner and then - Oh, before that Grondal

'Knafahólar' (*Saga-steads* 19) (6 August 1897)

came to see sketches and brought me his great work specially illuminated and inscribed and I gave him some paints; in the afternoon the editor of Isafold the chief paper came to interview me and see sketches. Now he's gone and I finish hurriedly.

We saw Geyser spout, not very high - and went on to Haukadalr where Ari Froði lived - and deciphered an inscription on the church and got coffee, and had a tipsy guide back - the only person who was discontented with his pay. We rode in the twilight to Muli - a nice farm kept by an old widow - a farm which the King of Denmark inspected when he came to Iceland in 1874. We had good lodging, and next day a wet and tedious ride through clay mud* and what ought to be fine scenery to Thingvellir - but stopped at a poor farm before it, roused the farmer and slept in an outhouse very dirty and yet glad of shelter as it was dark and horses tired. Next day crept to Thingvellir, the famous place of Althing in old times - photographed in good sunshine and sketched all that day and next: sold horses to the parson, and borrowed horses and his boy to ride here, which we did in 5½ hours on a good road going delightfully trot and gallop after so many days creeping over mires and mud. It was comfortable to be in this good hotel again, and we spent a pleasant evening at Arni Thorsteinsson's; and had a good cigar and nice Iceland liqueur and talk

'Fellsmúli - Earthquake crack
Síra Einar & Jón Stefánsson'

Abbot Hall

'Ferry on the Thjórsá - ferryman trying to drive horses into deep water'

Abbot Hall

'Viktoria Guðmundsdóttir of Thjórsárholt'

in both tongues, and a cosy night after it: glad to be almost near home again. It has been a great grind, with much that was not enjoyment, and much that was. We went aboard Thyra last night and engaged a cabin, almost the last that was vacant: which will be our abode for a fortnight, into the Arctic Circle and back to Leith. I am glad that the end of the labour is coming, but if you saw how surprised and pleased all these good people are at the results, you would feel with me that it's not wasted, though I dare say the sketches aren't great art or even good sketches. But they are portraits of interesting places, and fine scenery: with colour in it. Now I hear that Guðmundur Magnússon the chief doctor of Iceland is here; J.S. has taken sketches down again to show and I must follow. We go aboard soon - and so I may as well end with dearest love to you all. Your W.G.C.

Teresa Smith

'Family of Thjórsárholt'

Notes: This whole letter tends to be cramped and difficult to read.

1 When he got to Leith W.G.C. found instructions to shave off his beard before arriving home.
2 Miss Bownass, the Coniston postmistress.
3 'mud' ? - the first attempt at reading suggested 'sand'.
4 'Breiðabolstaðr' - word blotted in the middle.
5 'Raven the tailor' - John Raven the Coniston village tailor.
6 The 6th of August was W.G.C.'s 43rd birthday.
7 Ecclesiasticus 45.18. (Apocrypha).

Abbot Hall

'Thingbrekka and ancient booths' (*Saga-steads* 14) (10 August 1897)

'The Parliament of Ancient Iceland'

Abbot Hall

'Öxará', *Saga-steads* 9 10 August 1897

Abbot Hall

'The "Lögberg" looking North' (*Saga-steads* 11) (11 August 1897)

Abbot Hall

Abbot Hall

‘Gjá of Lögberg’

Abbot Hall

‘Snorrabuð’

Abbot Hall

‘Almannagjá’

Abbot Hall

‘Öxarárfoss’

Abbot Hall

‘Öxarárfoss’

Abbot Hall

'Öxará (Execution pool)'

Abbot Hall

'W.G.C.'

Abbot Hall

'Dr JS and the boy'

Abbot Hall

'W.G.C.'

From ***Nothing Much,*** August 1897

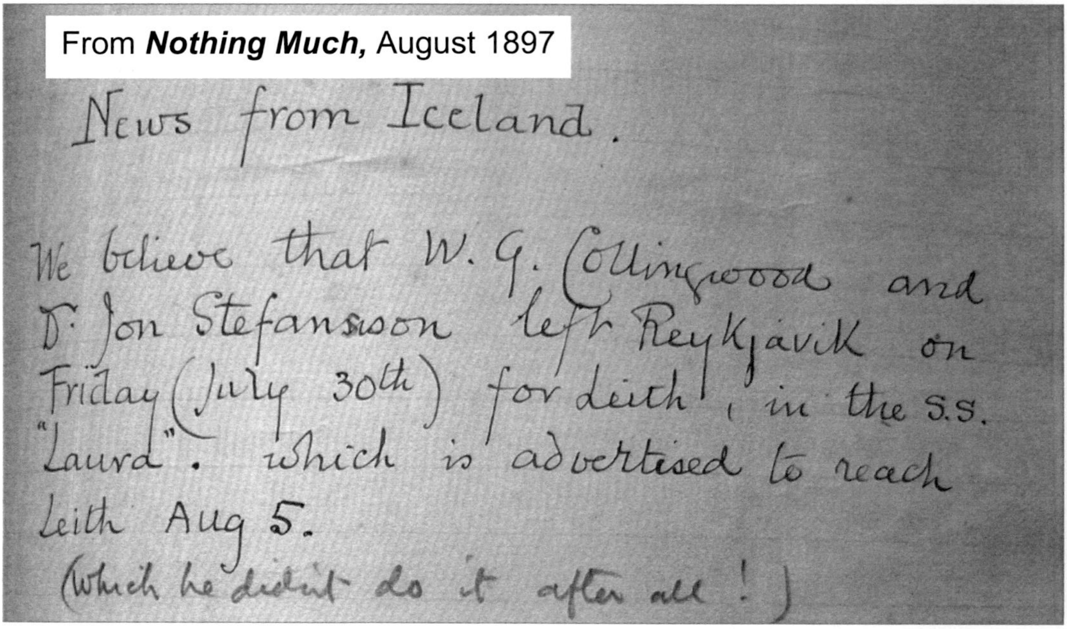

News from Iceland.

We believe that W. G. Collingwood and Dr Jon Stefansson left Reykjavik on Friday (July 30th) for Leith, in the S.S. "Laura". which is advertised to reach Leith Aug 5.

(which he didn't do it after all!)

Abbot Hall

Paintings of Iceland, a most delightful guest

Interview with W.G. Collingwood in the newspaper ***Ísafold*** on 18th of August 1897, by the co-editor of the paper, Einar Hjörleifsson (Kvaran), author.

Translated by Ida Talling

Our country has this year received a delightful guest, Mr Collingwood, the author, archaeologist, and painter. This summer he has been travelling the country with Dr Jón Stefánsson. The two companions travelled through the South to Markarfljót, all of the western part except for Westfjords, and Húnavatnssýsla. On Saturday night they started the trip on the SS *Thyra*, sailing north, intending to go to Skagafjörður and from there further east. We caught up with Mr Collingwood just before boarding the ship. We asked him if he had accomplished much this summer, and painted many pictures?

'About 250', he said, 'mostly colour', but he expected the number to rise to 300 by the end. They are, of course, not fully finished, he would do that when he arrives in London, and exhibit them for some time. Originally he only intended to paint the saga-steads. But in the end he found so many other places irresistible. His plan is to publish the pictures, preferably in colour, in many books. Abstracts from the sagas, covering the places he painted, will accompany the pictures, written by Jón Stefánsson.

'Do you think that Iceland will be a big tourist country in the future?'

'No doubt about that. The only thing preventing this is lack of information about this country. Only a few persons know about Reykjavík, Þingvellir and Geysir and not much more. But the traveller sees little of the real country. It has been shown that more knowledge will encourage more tourists. The travellers are getting tired of Switzerland and Norway which are not equal to the sights of this country.'

We now started to talk about specific places he had visited in this country. I understood that Collingwood was most impressed with Fljótshlíð, Gilsfjörður, the view from Stóra Borg in Húnavatnssýsla and Vatnsdalur but still above all of these were several places under Snæfellsjökull. Generally, most places had their own special beauty. It was obvious, that he had a trained eye to find what is beautiful.

We asked him also if he had been disappointed about Laxárdalur in Dalasýsla, considering the powerful saga which happened there. 'Not at all.' he said. 'The view to the mountains is not great, but the river with its riverbanks has many beautiful places. The valley is similar in character to the Scottish valleys, especially those where the epic poems of Scotland originated.' He had painted many pictures in Laxárdalur.

We returned to the expected increase in travellers to our country. 'The conditions for this increase' said Mr Collingwood 'would depend on specific arrangements here to receive foreigners. Do not misunderstand me, I had nothing to complain about. The hospitality shown to me everywhere was matchless. It has been excellent, even in the poorest huts. I was everywhere offered the best available on the farms. In many places I did not dare to offer money. I was received in such a way that I understood that I would offend them if I offered to pay. Many an offer to pay was refused. I did not miss the hotels, but the general public could not travel in this way. The tourist industry could not cope with a large increase in numbers. It is necessary to build hotels in many places in the country; keep them open in the summer, but close them during the winter, as is the custom in other countries. Arrangements need to be made for the travellers to amuse themselves and enjoy the beauty of nature. For example, there are no boats available to rent on Þingvallavatn but people would stay here for weeks if they could amuse themselves on the lake. And now there is a good access road there is no longer any possible excuse for delaying building a hotel there'.

We acknowledged this, but pointed out the difficulty in building reasonably good hotels in the countryside where the financial reward was uncertain, at least in the beginning. 'That is true' he said 'But you should accept that this will happen as this is a financial growth area and if the Icelanders do not do this the English will, and pocket the proceeds. It won't be me - this is not my profession, but as soon as a moneyed English gentleman in the travel industry comes he will see the potential for tourists to flock here from other nations once they learn what they can experience here. So he will take advantage of this and build hotels and advertise'.

Mr Collingwood had done few archaeological investigations here - his energy went into his pictures - but he did excavate the grave of Guðrún Ósvífrsdóttir at Helgafell. The grave had a wall of stone and certain traces all pointed to it being from the 11th century. He found a few iron parts but, as expected, nothing of precious metal, since Guðrún was a nun when she died[1]. He spoke very favourably of most Icelanders, but he could not help but criticize the way old tombstones were treated in Iceland as well as other things from bygone eras. The Skálholt stones were all broken up, the same story in many other places. When Collingwood arrived at one rectory, a tombstone from 1616 in the churchyard was being used for a new grave. He would not tell where this had happened. 'The Icelanders complain that foreigners export Icelandic antiquities. Just seeing how little the Icelanders care in such matters, is a reason for foreigners to covet such objects of antiquity.'

At the end of our conversation, Mr Collingwood showed us his pictures and only the lack of time spoilt our pleasure. He had taken great pains to portray the glorious brilliance of colour of the sky and mountains in Iceland. His sunset pictures were splendid and especially beautiful but we only had a quick view. There is no doubt that if Mr Collingwood's prophecy about the tourist influx is fulfilled it will owe a great deal and be thanks to his pictures.

R.G. Collingwood Society

'Helgafell', *Saga-steads* 79 (16 June 1897)

1 She was not a nun but a female anchoress or hermit.

Home on the SS *Thyra*

14 to 29 August 1897

LETTERS FROM ICELAND - the last of the series

To: William Collingwood, at Bristol

Leith
Sunday aftn
Aug 29/97[1]

My dear Father

We have arrived all right - much later than we expected - the Thyra detained by strong head winds and overloading.

I don't know when I shall get home - tomorrow sometime - but we are so far safely and well.

With love to Ruthie[2]

Your affn. son

W. G. C.

Notes:

1 Date written in pencil in William Collingwood's handwriting.

2 W.G.C's sister Ruth who kept house for her father.

Postscript: Some days later a letter was written to The Scotsman by W.G. Collingwood noting that on Sunday 29th of August there were no postage stamps available at Leith Post Office.

Abbot Hall

'Patreksfjörð' (*Saga-steads* 91) (16 August 1897)

Abbot Hall

'Gísli's Haukadalr' 17 August 1897

Abbot Hall

'From the bows'

Abbot Hall

'Second Class'

Teresa Smith

'Dr.J.S.& M. Duvau'

Abbot Hall

Abbot Hall

Abbot Hall

'Færoe men'

Abbot Hall

'Prof. Krabbe'

Abbot Hall

'E. Walthew Haigh'

Sea Captain?

'He would have made a fine soldier, and the proudest moment of his life, he used to say, was when on his way back from Iceland in 1897, bronzed and bearded, a pilot took him for captain of the ship.'

This quotation from W.G. Collingwood's obituary in the CWAAS *Transactions (CW2 xxxiii*, 1933, 308-312) shows the satisfaction that W.G.C. felt after his adventures. The picture by W.G.C. shown here is entitled 'Self Portrait' ('Sea Captain'). It is an oil on canvas painting (60.6 x 50.6 cm) and was recently given to Abbot Hall Art Gallery in Kendal as part of the Janet Gnosspelius bequest. Janet died in July 2010, the only child of Barbara Crystal Collingwood and Oscar Gnosspelius, a pioneer of aviation on Windermere. Janet became an architect in Liverpool but her family home was in Coniston. She had been amassing material for a biography of W.G.C. Teresa Smith 'whooped with delight' when she found the picture in Janet's roof.

Abbot Hall

'Sea Captain' - self-portrait

Abbot Hall

'In the Arctic sea, whales & north east point of Iceland' (23 August 1897)

Jón Stefánsson's Account of the Pilgrimage

from his Autobiography ***Úti í Heimi* (abroad)**

Bókfellsútgáfan h.f., Reykjavík, 1949, pages 118-123.

Translated by Ida Talling

W.G. Collingwood was a painter and archaeologist who lived by Lake Coniston[1] in North West England, in the Lake District (Lakeland), famous for its beauty. It has many small lakes, with mountains between them. Various Scandinavian local names occur there.

Collingwood gave a lecture to the Viking Society on Scandinavian names in that area. He then invited me to visit and stay with them for a while during the summertime. He had the idea that we should translate *Kormáks saga* together. I agreed to that plan. We found it very difficult to translate the poems in such a way as to be enjoyed by the British. We made many attempts, and at last we succeeded in attaining some of the splendid gift of poetry and aesthetic splendour of the kenning. Collingwood put, in the beginning of the book, a picture of Steingerðr, peeping into the drinking room - under Hagbarðr's head, carved on the door post, but Kormákr sits inside drinking. Ursula, Collingwood's 15 year old daughter, was his model for Steingerðr. The translation and publication were well received.

Collingwood now decided to go to Iceland, travel widely in the country and paint as many of the famous Saga-steads as possible. He asked me to accompany him. I was very glad to do so and it resulted in this special trip of ours. We stepped ashore in Reykjavík and from there we travelled west to Stykkishólmur. We brought with us Kristian Kaalund's book on the Saga-steads in Iceland [*Bidrag til en historisk-topografisk beskrivelse af Island, 1877–1882*].

According to Guðbrandur Vigfússon, the ancestors of the most noble Irish-Icelandic families settled in Dalasýsla, and indeed we trace the beginning of historical writing in Iceland to them. Guðbrandur attributes this to the influence of stories and story-telling on the Irish. Verbal storytelling gives information on where in Helgafell the grave of Guðrún Ósvífrsdóttir is located. Collingwood had investigated several graves in North and North West England. Now he wanted to investigate Guðrún's grave. He very carefully loosened the topmost turf, and then, with great care, he put the soil underneath into buckets.

Dr Jón Stefánsson

1 Previously Thurstonwater (Þorsteinsvatn).

The lowermost layer was charcoal ash and one bead, possibly from a rosary. We gave the bead to a man in Stykkishólmur and asked him to send it to The National History Museum (Þjóðminjasafnið).

My father met us in Stykkishólmur. Daníel, the son of the great chieftain Árni Thorlacius, had married Anna, my father's sister. Anna and Daníel lived in the Norwegian House - ('Norskhús', in local slang), the largest house in Stykkishólmur. My father and I stayed with the couple. Möller, the pharmacist, had invited Collingwood and myself to stay with him, but Collingwood preferred to stay in a small hotel to avoid guests and feasts. When we arrived, Anna and David had moved to a small island with a large breeding place of Eider ducks, and there they studied the ducks in peace. They got together with the gentlefolks from the village to invite me and Collingwood onto this rocky island, Súgandisey, which forms the harbour of Stykkishólmur. We first had to climb the steep crag onto the island, and then an alfresco feast awaited us. There we sat in the sunshine with a horn of plenty and looked down upon Stykkishólmur. There were many speeches and the words were big, as is customary with the Icelanders, when they finally loosen their tongue-tied nature in a crowd. I had to be the interpreter as no one understood English.

Life and Death of Cormac the Skald

'Cormac sees Steingerd at the door'

Anna, my father's sister, was a poet, loved books, and well able as an author. She published chapters of autobiography in 'Eimreið' and amusing observations of the life of the Eider duck. When we left Stykkishólmur, she accompanied us a bit of the way and she gave me a beautiful gold ring, which had belonged to her father-in-law, Árni Thorlacius. Árni was most valiant and clever of men, on sea and land, but later in life he became an archaeologist, collected local (topographical) names from olden times and explained about *Eyrbyggja*. He lived in the Norwegian House, the tallest house in town, and he was also the tallest of men. He wrote many pieces for Jón Sigurðsson and was a great supporter of Jón. He supported Sigurður Breiðfjord, and helped him with reserve funds. Sigurður was sometimes called his court-poet. Árni was considered a great wrestler and one of the greatest sea-heroes of his time in the

Teresa Smith

'Súgandisey from Stykkishólmur'

western part of Iceland, - and there were many stories about him from this region in the last third of the 19th century. Knowledgeable men have told me that since the saga age no other Icelander has excelled so in both physical and mental agility. He was open-handed with poor people and helpful to people in trouble. His compatriots spoke about him in the same way as about Jón Sigurðsson, and called him an honour for Iceland. Jón Sigurðsson had also valued him and could not praise him enough.

Teresa Smith

'Magnús Blöndal and Jón Stefánsson at dinner'

Now we rode with my father to Grundarfjörður, and were of course, well received there. My father bought two good horses for us and they proved very well on our trips in the North and South of Iceland. We were mounted and riding every day for three months, early morning to late at night. What we most of all enjoyed was a heaped plateful of skyr with sugar and cream in the morning, before leaving. We then did not need anything till we again ate skyr in the evening in the hotel.

This reminded me of the story which the most eminent comparative language expert Rasmus Chr. Rask told about skyr. He had spent two winters in Iceland, and got used to skyr, and he spoke Icelandic so well, he was mistaken for an Icelander. The Royal Danish Academy of Science then sent him to India and Persia to collect old manuscripts. Once, when travelling in the mountain area of Persia, he was offered a dish, very similar to skyr. He asked for the Persian name of this dish, Sgirr, - or something like that was what I heard. He threw his hands up in delight. Now here was the proof of the relationship between Iceland and Persia from way back in time. Forefathers of the Scandinavians and the forefathers of the Persian people had many thousands of years ago been nomadic tribes in Middle Asia, moving with their grazing herds and subsisting on skyr. They had a common vocabulary.

On our trips, Collingwood and I never spent the night under the stars, except for one night at Holtavörðuheiði. We then used the saddles as pillows, and put on all our coats and raincoats. The horses were grazing nearby - not tied. The hospitality was so great, nobody would accept payment. It was considered important to get pictures of the saga-steads. We often gave some money secretly to the children and Collingwood sometimes painted a picture of their child to give to the parent. Now they are of great value. The worst place we visited was an unnamed rectory. Disorder everywhere, dilapidated inside and outside. We decided not to stop at this rectory, went to a nearby farm and a much better place.

We stopped by to visit the scholar, Reverend Þorvaldur at Melstaður. His table was laden with books, magazines, left-over-food, but we very much enjoyed our conversation with Reverend Þorvaldur. Once two English generals from Egypt visited him. They lived in Cairo. The clergyman started to talk about some temples in that town, and the street and squares adjacent to them. The generals said he had got it all wrong. Reverend Þorvaldur then fetched some old and new maps of Cairo and showed the generals that he was right, and they were wrong. A country bumpkin clergyman on a remote island, near the arctic circle, knew more about their town, where they had lived the last ten years, than they did.

Reverend Þorvaldur published in Copenhagen *Remnants of ancient Christian lore*, the oldest Icelandic book of this kind. He accomplished this writing in a masterly fashion. It was a crime to force such a man to a lowly job in the country. In 1747, Finnur Jónsson, later bishop, was the clergyman in Reykholt. Harboe bypassed him for the nomination to the bishopric of Skálholt, and appointed Ólafur Gíslason as bishop. Harboe did this in order to let Finnur devote all his time to write *The History of the Icelandic Church*, not because he considered him less suitable as bishop than Ólafur. The Church Ministry then arranged for Finnur to get the same salary for composing the church history. The Danish Magistrate seemed to be more supportive towards Icelandic scholars than the Icelanders themselves at the end of the 19th century and the first decade of the 20th century.

We sold the horses at the end of our trip at the same price as we had paid earlier. Einar Hjörleifsson wrote a long article in *Ísafold* about the trip and praised the work and enthusiasm of Collingwood. The travel partners, Collingwood and I, parted company in Edinburgh. He went home to Coniston and I went to London.

We then cooperated on a book: *A Pilgrimage to the Saga-steads of Iceland*. The greater part of the work was carried out by Collingwood because he supervised the printing in the Lake District. His pictures were in colour, and he had to draw them all again in black and white, because of the cost of colour printing. I worked my part of the deal in London. The price of the book was 30 shillings, the issue was therefore small - only 500 copies. An Icelandic bookseller in Winnipeg asked for 50 copies. He must have sold these as none were returned. He wrote to us that the buyers were reluctant to pay and gave many excuses and quibbles. We never received any money from him. A British lawyer advised us not to sue him, but the amount was still £75. There are indeed black sheep in a herd. The book sold well in England and Iceland. F. York Powell, Guðbrandur Vigfússon's co-worker, wrote an excellent review in the *Manchester Guardian*, a newspaper which comes close to *The Times* in fame.

Collingwood had painted about 350 pictures of the saga-steads in Iceland. The Viking Society gave a dinner for him. Viscount Bryce was the chairman and gave an excellent speech about the trip. The pictures hung in the Dining Room. After that, two exhibitions were held in London and a few were sold.

When Ásgeir Ásgeirsson was Prime Minister, I wrote a letter to him on behalf of Collingwood and emphasized the importance for Iceland to get possession of the whole collection of the saga-stead pictures; they showed the condition of the saga-steads before the end of the 19th century. Ásgeir answered that he agreed with me. He also pointed out that because of financial difficulties, he had no money to spare to buy the pictures. Ásgeir never asked for the price, and maybe I should not have told him about it anyway, but my idea was that the government should approach Collingwood directly. Thus my dear friend Collingwood thought that the Icelandic government had no interest in acquiring the pictures. He might perhaps even have donated them, had he known that the government was temporarily short of money but interested to get them. Thus foundered the possibility for Iceland to own this very exceptional collection of the saga-steads and now the pictures are scattered all over the world.

Collingwood is the author of a remarkable book *Scandinavian Britain*. He had investigated all Scandinavian objects of antiquity and found gravestones from the early part of the 12th century in Lancashire – with Scandinavian characters. He therefore concluded that the Scandinavian language had been spoken by the people who put up the gravestones in the beginning of the

12th century.

Collingwood hailed from a remarkable English family. When Nelson fell in the battle of Trafalgar, Admiral Collingwood, the ancestor of our painter and scholar, took control and won the big victory over the French and Spanish navies. This victory saved England, as Napoleon was well prepared to cross the Channel and invade England[2].

The son of Collingwood, the traveller in Iceland, became the Waynflete Professor of Metaphysical Philosophy at Oxford University. He wrote several remarkable books, but died young in age [Eds: he died in 1943, aged 52]. Collingwood's daughters married as follows: one a Swedish person, living in his house in the Lake District; the second an artist from Aleppo and Damascus in Syria; the third a clergyman from the home pastures. In the earlier part of his life, Collingwood was a secretary to Ruskin, the famous aesthete, and Collingwood wrote the best biography of him. Collingwood died in 1932. He was a good-looking man, gentle and everybody's darling. He was Professor of Fine Art at Reading University from 1907-11.

---

2 Eds. Extensive research has failed to find a family link with Admiral Lord Cuthbert Collingwood. See *A Lakeland Saga* by Jeremy Collingwood, p.9 (Sigma Leisure, 2012).

Obituary for Dr Jón Stefánsson

by Eiríkur Benedikz

Viking Society *Saga-Book* **13,** 364-5 (1952-3)

Dr. Jón Stefánsson, one of the founder members of the Viking Society (or Viking Club as it was first called) died in Reykjavík on the 20th July, 1952.

Dr. Stefánsson was born in Iceland on 4th November, 1862. He was educated at the Reykjavík Grammar School and went afterwards to the University of Copenhagen where he studied English Language and Literature under Professor George Stephens.

During his undergraduate days he was awarded the University's Gold Medal for an essay on dialects in Wycliffe's Bible translation. In 1889 he graduated as M.A. and two years later the University accepted his doctor's thesis on Robert Browning (*Robert Browning* (1812-1889); *et literaturbillede fra det moderne England*). Dr. Stefánsson's book on Browning was one of the first serious attempts to make this poet known to the literary public of the Scandinavian countries.

At about this time the chair of English in the University of Copenhagen became vacant and it was generally considered that Dr. Stefánsson would be appointed to this post. This was, however, not to be, as Dr. Otto Jespersen, who had attacked Dr. Stefánsson's book on Browning just before a decision was made on the appointment, obtained the post.

Shortly after Professor Jespersen's appointment Dr. Stefánsson left Copenhagen and went to London where he was to spend more than fifty years of his life with short breaks only. In London he soon became acquainted with many well-known scholars, especially those who were interested in Icelandic literature and language. Among these were William Morris, Sir Israel Gollancz, W. P. Ker, Viscount Bryce and A. W. Johnstone, the founder and secretary of the Viking Society.

During his long stay in London Dr. Stefánsson never had any permanent post, except that he was for a few years lecturer in Icelandic and Danish at King's College. In fact I do not think it suited his temperament to be tied down to an office or a teaching post. He had to be free to work on what interested him most at the time and to do it in his own way. Although Dr. Stefánsson undoubtedly acquired a vast amount of learning during his long life of research work in the British Museum, his printed works are surprisingly few. They mostly consist of articles in newspapers and periodicals, British, Scandinavian, French and German. In 1899 he published, in collaboration with W.G. Collingwood, a book called *A Pilgrimage to the Saga-steads of Iceland*. Dr. Stefánsson was responsible for the text but the illustrations were by Collingwood.

His largest printed work, apart from his memoirs, appeared in 1916, in the Stories of Nations series called *Denmark and Sweden with Iceland and Finland*. In addition to these he left behind him in MS a *History of Iceland* in English.

In 1918 Dr. Stefánsson married a French widow [Eds: Claire Adrienne de Chazal] from Mauritius. Shortly after the wedding they went to live there, but it seemed as if he could not settle away from London so they parted and he returned to his studies at the British Museum. Here he lived until late in the year 1948 when he went back to Reykjavík to spend there the last few years of his life. In 1949 his memoirs were published in Reykjavík, under the title *Úti í Heimi*.

Appendix 1: The Paintings of Iceland by W.G. Collingwood

During his journey round Iceland, W.G. Collingwood did about 300 watercolours and sketches and more back home. There are three categories of his Icelandic paintings and drawings.

The first category are the original paintings he made during his 1897 tour. His hand-written list of these 'Sketches in Iceland' is shown on pages 132 and 133. Some of the existing paintings are signed and precisely dated, with or without a title, and are likely be these originals.

Collingwood was a professional artist and when he returned home, he exhibited his paintings at selling exhibitions. He painted extra colour copies of his sketches, particularly of those he sold. These were normally in watercolour but include his most famous oil painting 'The Icelandic Parliament at Thingvellir', which is now in the British Museum (see page 115). These new versions form the second category.

The final category are the black and white drawings and monochrome paintings specifically done for the illustrations in *A Pilgrimage to the Saga-steads of Iceland* and in *Cormac the Skald*. There are also 13 colour paintings printed in *Saga-steads* - an innovation in 1899. A numbered list of these illustrations, on pages 134 and 135, gives the place-name or subject as given in *Saga-steads* and their current known location - in Þjóðminjasafn Íslands (Reykjavík), Abbot Hall, (Kendal) or the R.G. Collingwood Society archive (Cardiff).

After his death, little was known about the original paintings. It is due to the untiring efforts of the English benefactor Mark Watson that most of the paintings are now in Þjóðminjasafn Íslands, as described by Janet Gnosspelius in her Introduction. A further 38 paintings and drawings were left by the late well-known Icelandic Jesuit Father Jón Sveinsson (1857-1944), author of the renowned *Nonni* books which have been translated into over 30 languages. These were also donated to the National Museum of Iceland. In 1988 Haraldur Hannesson published the magnificent book, *Fegurð Íslands og fornir sögustaðir* (Reykjavík, 1988) with 163 paintings from Reykjavík, many photographs and an Icelandic translation of Collingwood's *Letters from Iceland*. The paintings are shown on the Museum's web-site: www.ljosmyndasafnislands.is/ljosmyndir/gallery.asp?categoryid=197.

Another 32 Icelandic paintings and drawings were donated to the Collingwood archive in the Abbot Hall Art Gallery (Lakeland Arts Trust), Kendal, Cumbria, England, by Janet Gnosspelius, together with the original Letters from Iceland, his Diaries, the original manuscript of *Saga-steads* and many other documents (reference: AH/2510/83/WGC). The paintings reproduced in this book are listed on page 136.

Seven more paintings, originally given to Jón Stefánsson by Collingwood, were located in Denmark in 2001 (see pages 59 - 65).

Recently a further 61 drawings and paintings were left by Janet Gnosspelius to the R.G. Collingwood Society in Cardiff University. Some 57 of these are beautiful black and white drawings and paintings done for *Saga-steads* (see pages 134 and 135) along with 2 watercolours and 2 black and white drawings done for *Cormac the Skald*. Others may well be found.

One of our aims here is to complement the paintings located in Iceland and illustrated in *Fegurð Íslands og fornir sögustaðir* with W.G. Collingwood's previously unknown paintings and drawings held in UK archives. We have also included some of the original *Saga-steads* drawings from Cardiff where they match the paintings or are of special interest, as shown on page 136.

W.G. Collingwood's sketches in Iceland 1897

Hand-written list in Abbot Hall, Kendal.

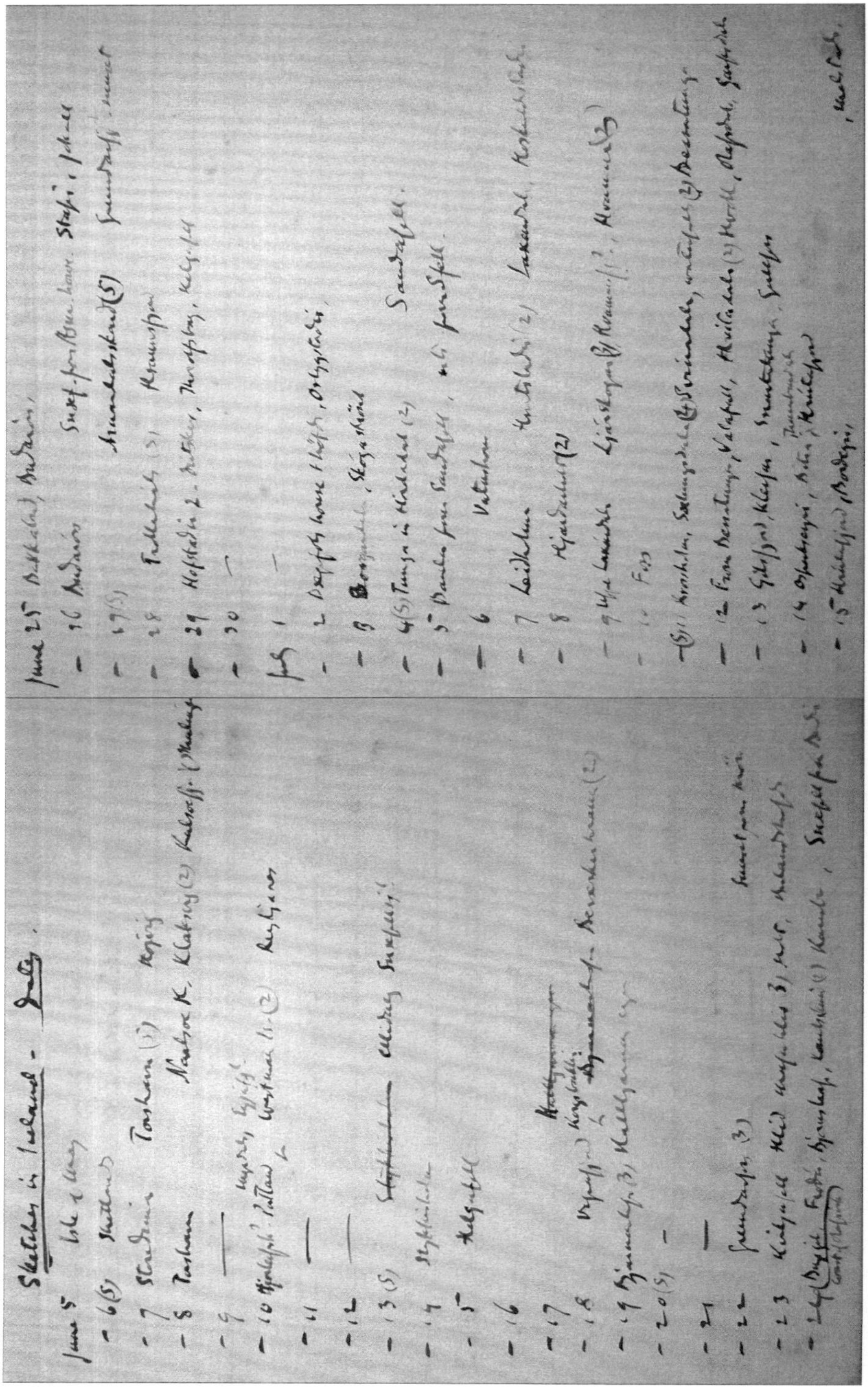

Abbot Hall

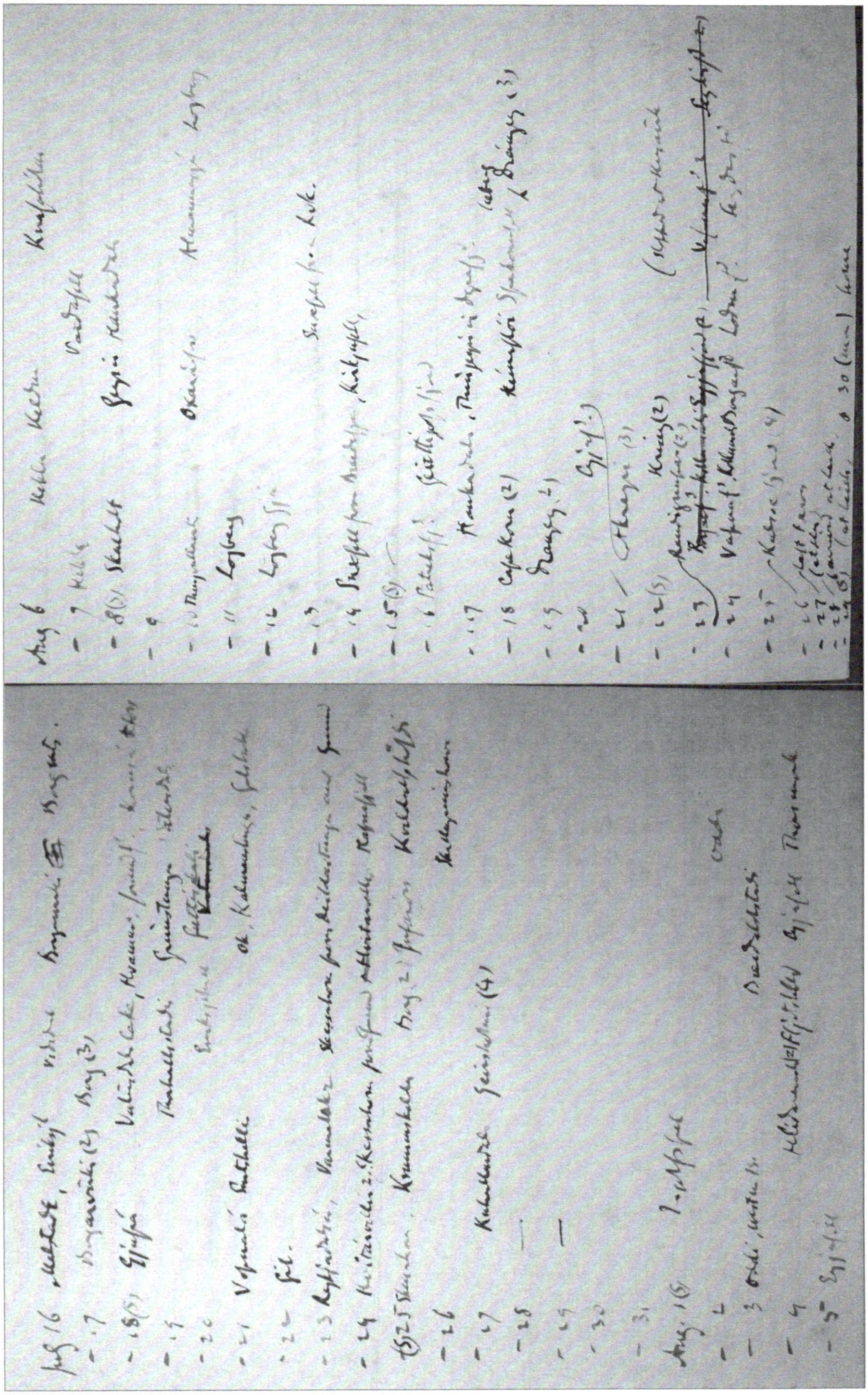

Abbot Hall

A Pilgrimage to the Saga-steads of Iceland: Illustrations

The numbered illustrations and their titles, as printed in *Saga-steads,* are listed below, including 13 in colour. The black and white or monochrome illustrations were drawn specifically for *Saga-steads* from a selection of the original watercolours, though number 67 'Hrauns-fjord' is dated 28 June 1897, which may indicate that it was done in Iceland. Many of these drawings for *Saga-steads* are now in Þjóðminjasafn Íslands, Reykjavík (labelled **R**), in Abbot Hall, Kendal **(K)** or in the R.G. Collingwood Society archive in Cardiff (**C**), as shown below. Many of the original colour paintings and sketches on which they are based are also in these archives or in private ownership.

The very small black numbers on the map from *Saga-steads* on page 140, and throughout this book, show the sites where the original sketches were done.

Sixteen of the *Saga-steads* illustrations were also reproduced in *The Life and Death of Cormac the Skald* in 1902 (marked *), along with six new illustrations as listed.

List of paintings

The paintings in this book by W.G. Collingwood are listed below with their original titles. The corresponding illustration numbers in *Saga-steads* are given as S+number (in brackets unless it is the original illustration used, see pages 134 and 135). The date when the site was visited is in the figure captions, in brackets unless the date is on the painting itself which may indicate it was painted in Iceland at the time. Some paintings from *Nothing Much* are also listed.

Appendix 2: W.G. Collingwood's Icelandic Photographs

As well as a professional artist, Collingwood was also a pioneering photographer. In 1897 he took a small Kodak camera and 5 boxes of films with him to Iceland. The camera was a 'Pocket Kodak' which was first produced in 1895 (price $5) by the Eastman Kodak Co. in Rochester, New York and imported into the UK for sale by Kodak Ltd. It was of the box form type, measuring 3" x $2\frac{1}{4}$" x 4", slipping easily into an ordinary coat pocket. It used a newly developed paper-backed roll film, type 102, producing twelve $1\frac{1}{2}$" x 2" negatives on a daylight-loading spool with a ratchet spool movement. It incorporated a small 'red' window through which the exposure number could be read. The camera design was modified a number of times and it remained in production until 1900. Although the pictures are small, the Pocket Kodak was enormously popular and about 147,000 were made.[1]

Collingwood's own original photographic album of their Pilgrimage is in Abbot Hall Art Gallery, Kendal. The first three pages show local photographs of **Lanehead Garden** (containing 6 photos) followed by two pages on **Peel Island** near Barrow (10 photos). It then has pages headed **Færoes** (6); **Torshavn** (6); **Vestmannaeyjar** (5); **(Westman Islands)** (5); **Reykjavík** (4); **Reykjavík** (5, shown here); **Snæfellsnes** (7); **Snæfellsnes** (8); **Sauðafell** (9); **Bær** (7); **Borðeyri** (4) and **Borgarvirki** (2); **Borg** (7); **Vatnsdalr** (8); **Grimstungu-heiði** (8); **Surts-hellir** (two pages: 7 and 4); **Lava field of the Hvítá at Gilsbakki** (7); **Hvítá** (6); **Kálfholt** (6); **Hliðarendi** (4); **Fellsmúli Earthquake cracks** (5); **Thjórsá** (5); **Thingvellir** (8); **Almannagjá** (8); **Back to Reykjavík** (6); **On board the Thyra** (6); and finally two more pages **on the Thyra** (7 and 7).

Abbot Hall

Photographic album page on Reykjavík

All the pages and photographs were annotated and labelled in pencil by Collingwood himself. There are a total of 145 Icelandic photographs and another 32 taken en route. A set of these photographs is also in Þjóðminjasafn Íslands, Reykjavík.

Teresa Smith recently found some of the original negatives in the boxes of archive material from Janet Gnosspelius. Despite their age, they are still in good condition.

We have used 72 photographs from the Abbot Hall album or scanned by George Smith from the original negatives to illustrate W.G. Collingwood's *Letters from Iceland.*

1 See http://www.earlyphotography.co.uk/site/entry_C447.html

Appendix 3: *A Pilgrimage to the Saga-steads of Iceland*

W.G. Collingwood and Jón Stefánsson (W. Holmes, Ulverston, 1899)

When Collingwood returned home, he began work on *A Pilgrimage to the Saga-steads of Iceland,* a travel book with a fully illustrated regional guide to the saga-sites of Iceland. It contains 13 of his colour paintings along with 139 in black and white, specifically repainted in monochrome or drawn in pen and ink. Most of the text was written in three weeks in November 1897. The book (500 copies) was published in 1899 by an Ulverston printer, William Holmes.[1] A facsimile copy is available.[2]

The original hand-written manuscript is in Abbot Hall Art Gallery, Kendal - extracts from the Preface are shown below.

'This is a picture book to illustrate the sagas of Iceland'

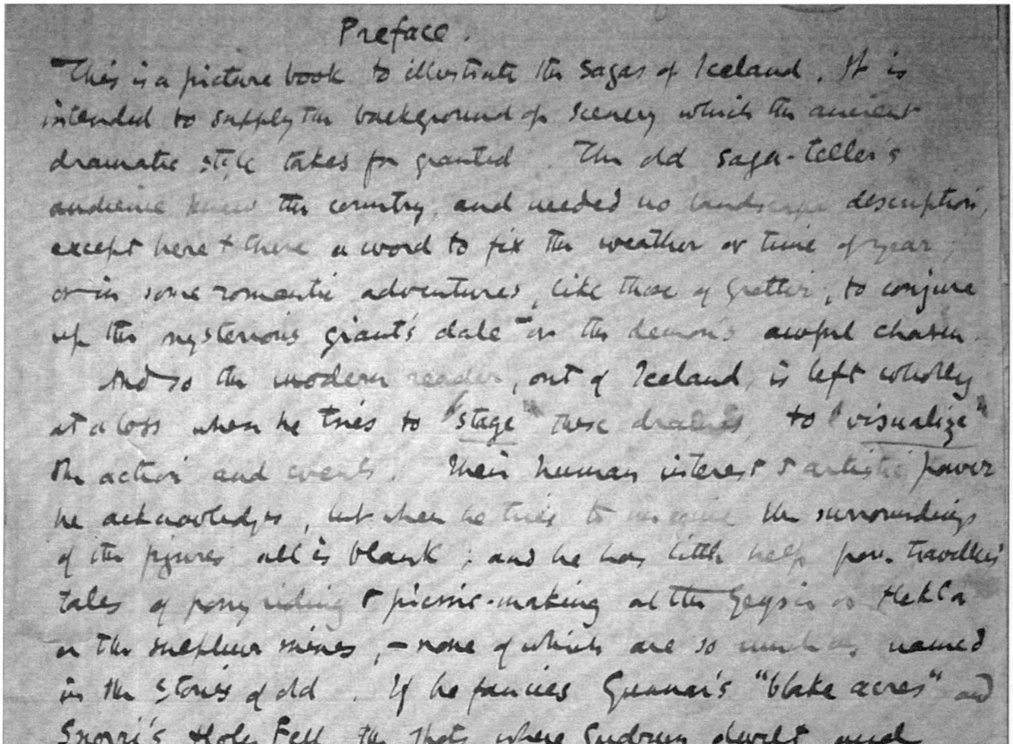
Preface.

This is a picture book to illustrate the Sagas of Iceland. It is intended to supply the background of scenery which the ancient dramatic style takes for granted. The old saga-teller's audience knew the country, and needed no landscape description, except here & there a word to fix the weather or time of year; or in some romantic adventures, like those of Grettir, to conjure up the mysterious giant's dale or the demon's awful chasm.

And so the modern reader, out of Iceland, is left wholly at a loss when he tries to "stage" these dramas, to "visualize" the action and events. Their human interest & artistic power he acknowledges, but when he tries to imagine the surroundings of the figures all is blank; and he has little help from travellers' tales of pony riding & picnic-making at the Geysir or Hekla or the sulphur mines, — none of which are so much as named in the stories of old. If he fancies Gunnar's "black acres" and Snorri's Holy Fell, the spots where Gudrun dwelt and

Abbot Hall

1 A full account of writing the book and its content is given by Townend, M, *The Vikings and Victorian Lakeland: The Norse Medievalism of W.G. Collingwood and his Contemporaries* (CWAAS Extra Series XXXIV, 2009).

2 *A Pilgrimage to the Saga-steads of Iceland* is available from the British Library, Historical Print Editions, published by Lightning Source UK Ltd (2011), ISBN 978-1241311452.

'While one of us drew'

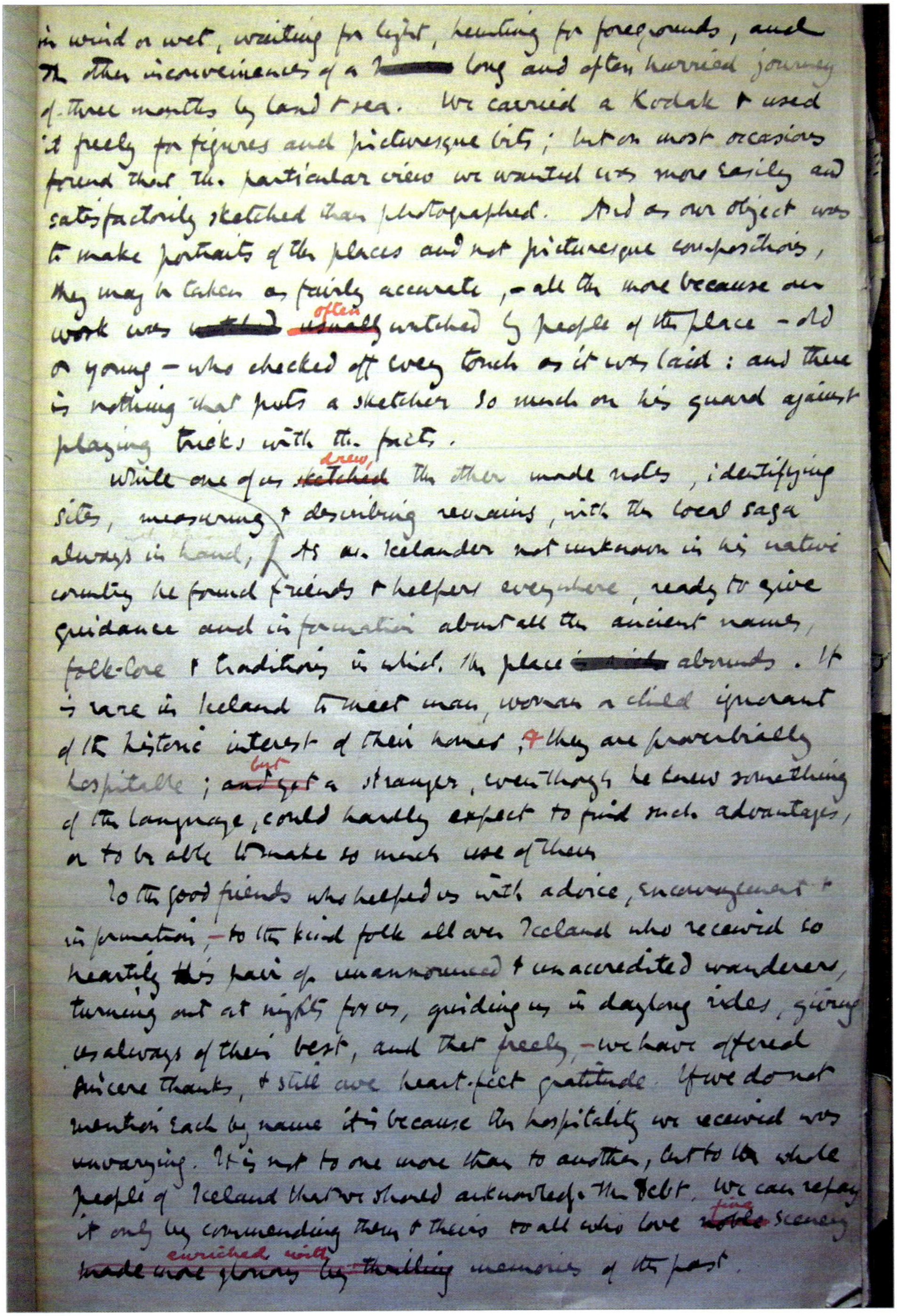

in wind or wet, waiting for light, hunting for foregrounds, and the other inconveniences of a [redacted] long and often hurried journey of three months by land & sea. We carried a Kodak & used it freely for figures and picturesque bits; but on most occasions found that the particular view we wanted was more easily and satisfactorily sketched than photographed. And as our object was to make portraits of the places and not picturesque compositions, they may be taken as fairly accurate, — all the more because our work was [redacted] ~~usually~~ often watched by people of the place — old & young — who checked off every touch as it was laid: and there is nothing that puts a sketcher so much on his guard against playing tricks with the facts.

While one of us ~~sketched~~ drew, the other made notes, identifying sites, measuring & describing remains, with the local saga always in hand. As an Icelander not unknown in his native country he found friends & helpers everywhere, ready to give guidance and information about all the ancient names, folk-lore & traditions in which the place [redacted] abounds. It is rare in Iceland to meet man, woman or child ignorant of the historic interest of their homes, & they are proverbially hospitable; ~~and yet~~ but a stranger, even though he knew something of the language, could hardly expect to find such advantages, or to be able to make so much use of them.

To the good friends who helped us with advice, encouragement & information, — to the kind folk all over Iceland who received so heartily this pair of unannounced & unaccredited wanderers, turning out at nights for us, guiding us in daylong rides, giving us always of their best, and that freely, — we have offered sincere thanks, & still owe heart-felt gratitude. If we do not mention each by name it is because the hospitality we received was unvarying. It is not to one more than to another, but to the whole people of Iceland that we should acknowledge the debt. We can repay it only by commending them & theirs to all who love ~~noble~~ fine scenery ~~made more glorious by thrilling~~ enriched with memories of the past.

Abbot Hall

The *Saga-steads* Map

The map of Iceland in *Saga-steads* below shows the sites of 151 illustrations (small numbers in black; see pages 16, 134 and 135). W.G. Collingwood and Jón Stefánsson set out to visit sites from many of the Icelandic sagas. The geographical regions where some of the sagas were set are shown below in red (Emily Lethbridge: http://sagasteads.blogspot.com/p/saga-steads-map.html).

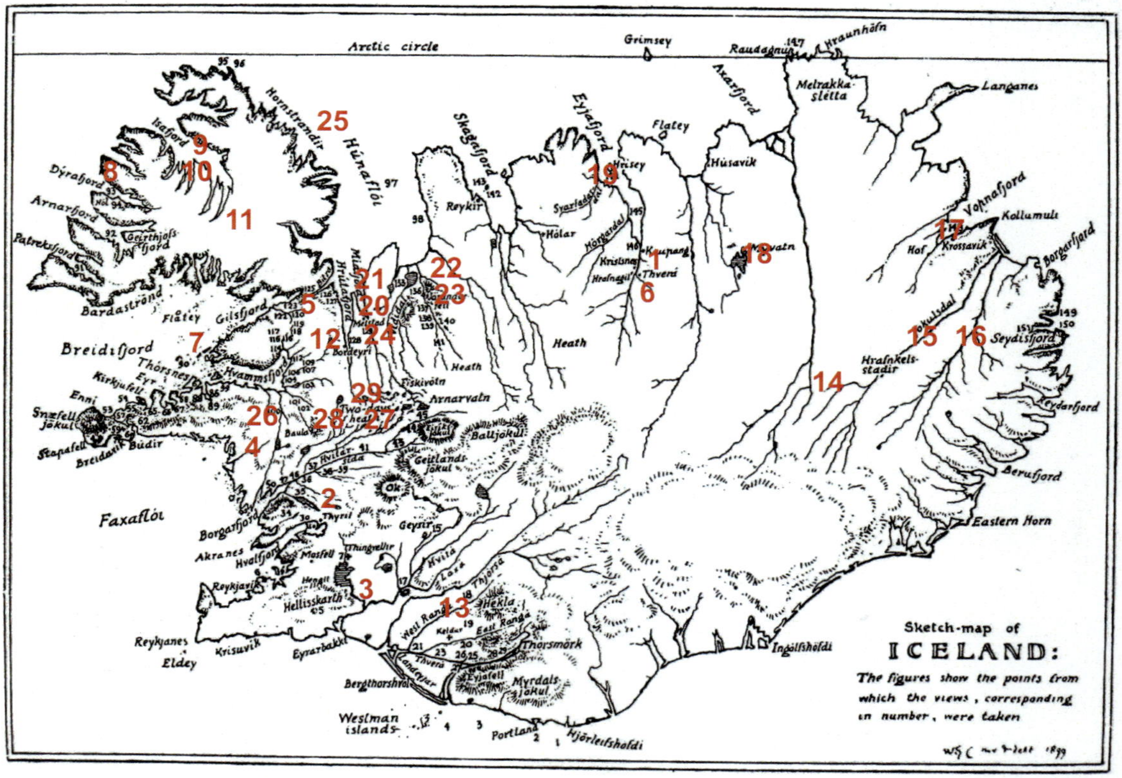

1. *Víga-Glúms saga*
2. *Harðar saga*
3. *Flóamanna saga*
4. *Egils saga*
5. *Laxdæla saga*
6. *Ljósvetninga saga*
7. *Eyrbyggja saga*
8. *Gísla saga*
9. *Fóstbræðra saga*
10. *Hávarðar saga*
11. *Gull-Þóris saga*
12. *Eiríks saga rauða*
13. *Njáls saga*
14. *Hrafnkels saga*
15. *Droplaugarsona saga*
16. *Flótsdæla saga*
17. *Vápnfirðinga saga*
18. *Reykdæla saga*
19. *Svarfdæla saga*
20. *Grettis saga*
21. *Bandamanna saga*
22. *Vatnsdæla saga*
23. *Hallfreðar saga*
24. *Kormáks saga*
25. *Finnboga saga*
26. *Bjarnar saga*
27. *Gunnlaugs saga*
28. *Hænsa-Þóris saga*
29. *Heiðarvíga saga*

Appendix 4:
‘People in Iceland to whom I must send something’ - W.G.C.’s Diary 16 November 1897

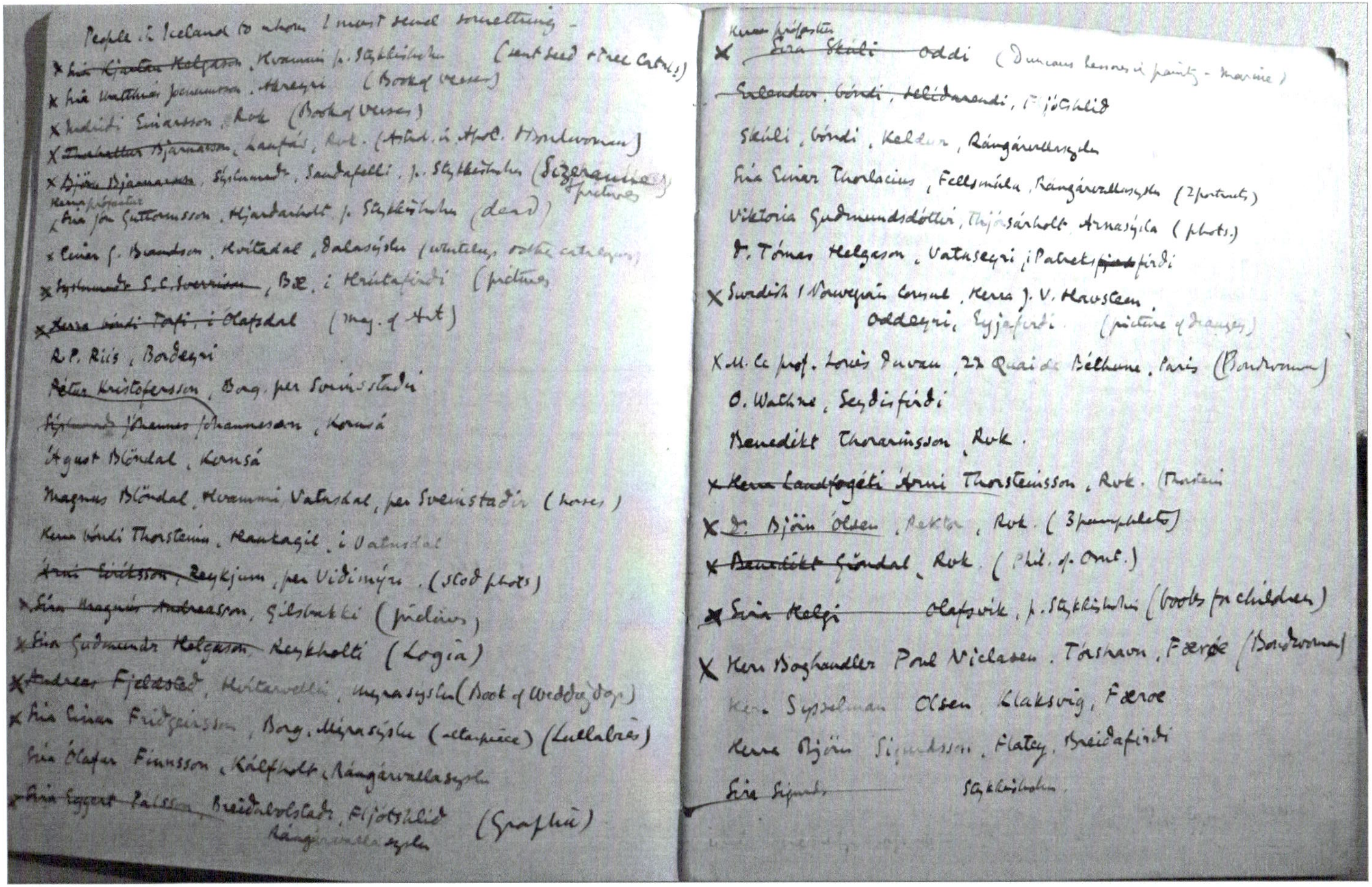

Abbot Hall

Appendix 5: Collingwood Family Tree

William Gershom Collingwood was the son of William Collingwood and his Swiss wife Maria Imhoff who had three children. Gershom married Edith Mary Isaac in 1883 and had four children, Dorothy (Dora), Barbara, Robin and Ursula, and eleven grandchildren, including Teresa Smith (née Collingwood) and Janet Gnosspelius, who have contributed to this book. His great-grandchildren are not shown on this family tree. **Jake Collingwood**

See also *Lakeland Saga* by Jeremy Collingwood (Sigma Leisure, 2012).

William COLLINGWOOD 1819-1903 = 1851 = **Maria Elizabeth IMHOFF 1826-1873**

William Gershom COLLINGWOOD 1854-1932 = 1883 = **Edith Mary ISAAC 1857-1928**

Ernest Haig Riddell ALTOUNYAN 1889-1962 = 1916 = **Dorothy (Dora) Susie COLLINGWOOD 1886-1964**

- **Barbara Harriet Taqui ALTOUNYAN (Mrs Stephens) 1917-2001**
- **Susan Arshalouis ALTOUNYAN (Mme Villard) 1919-2003**
- **Norah Mavis Araxi ALTOUNYAN (Mrs Guzelian) 1920-1998**
- **Roger Edward Collingwood ALTOUNYAN 1922-1987**
- **Brigit Mary Lucine ALTOUNYAN (Mrs Sanders) 1926-1999**

Oscar Theodor GNOSSPELIUS 1878-1953 = 1925 = **Barbara Crystal COLLINGWOOD 1887-1961**

- **Janet Barbara GNOSSPELIUS 1926-2010**

Ethel Winifred GRAHAM 1885-1973 = 1918 = **Robin George COLLINGWOOD 1889-1943** = 1942 = **Kathleen EDWARDES 1911-1980**

- **William Robert COLLINGWOOD 1919-1975**
- **Ursula Ruth COLLINGWOOD (Mrs Parry) 1921-1943**
- **Teresa COLLINGWOOD (Mrs Smith) 1941-**

Reginald Bertram LUARD-SELBY 1885-1951 = 1925 = **Ursula Mavis COLLINGWOOD 1891-1962**

- **Sara Dorothy LUARD-SELBY 1926-1988**
- **Philippa Mary LUARD-SELBY (Mrs Fothergill) 1928-**
- **Richard Collingwood LUARD-SELBY 1930-1933**

Appendix 6: W.G. Collingwood and the CWAAS

The artist and author William Gershom Collingwood is one of the most important figures in the history of the CWAAS. Born in Liverpool in 1854, Collingwood came to know the Lakes from an early age, often in the company of his father, the watercolour artist William Collingwood. Following education at the University of Oxford (where he came under the influence of John Ruskin) and the Slade School of Art, Collingwood married in 1883 and settled in the Lakes: first at Gillhead, on the eastern shore of Windermere, and then, from 1891 till his death, at Lanehead, a house on the eastern shore of Coniston Water, close to Ruskin's home at Brantwood. Collingwood had three daughters and a son, the philosopher and Roman historian R.G. Collingwood, also a key player in the Society's history.

W.G. Collingwood joined the CWAAS in 1887. His first appearance in the Society's *Transactions* was in 1892, when he illustrated a paper by his friend W.S. Calverley. His first article appeared in 1894, on 'Some Manx Names in Cumbria' [see page 20]. This illuminated Cumbria's Viking past by means of a comparison with place-names in Iceland and the Isle of Man. It was the first of over 60 articles published in the *Transactions*, along with innumerable minor notes, reports, reviews, and obituaries. The range of these articles was extraordinary: not just in the fields of Viking studies and medieval stone sculpture – the areas in which Collingwood's scholarship is best known – but also industrial archaeology, literary history, church dedications, prehistoric settlement, Quakers, packhorse bridges, and Arthurian folklore.

Collingwood was elected a Council member in 1896 and, in 1900, succeeded Chancellor Richard Saul Ferguson as the Editor of the Society's *Transactions*. He designed Ferguson's funerary monument, a striking Viking-style hogback still to be seen at Stanwix church in Carlisle, and wrote his obituary for the *Transactions*. This obituary clearly expresses Collingwood's own views, and could equally well be applied to himself: 'He was most practical of men, but understood better than most who call themselves practical the place of art and literature in civilized life; in other words, an all-round man such as we seldom meet [...] He was no Dry-as-dust, nor a dog-in-the-manger scholar, nor an exploiter of labour; but a born teacher who made antiquarian study popular without vulgarizing it, and brought it home to plain folks and into touch with modern life as only a master-mind could do.'

As Editor for 25 years, Collingwood put the *Transactions* on a new footing for quality and content, and he established it as an annual publication. He designed a new logo for the Society, in the form of a medieval seal (shown). In 1920 Collingwood became President, and ensured that the CWAAS continued to thrive. But a series of strokes meant that he had to step down, and resign just before his death in 1932. Collingwood's final book, in the year of his death, was a revised edition of his classic guide *The Lake Counties*. He dedicated the new edition to the CWAAS and the Lake Artists Society (which he founded in 1904): 'may they flourish and long survive their faithful servant'. Both flourishing societies owe a great deal to this remarkable man, and it is right that members of the CWAAS should remember and celebrate his achievement. **Matthew Townend**

(from the CWAAS *Newsletter* **63**, Spring 2010)

Appendix 7: Iceland in W.G. Collingwood's *Thorstein of the Mere*

[Note 1: The text is from Collingwood's first edition of 1895 (written before his visit to Iceland) with significant variants noted in the revised second edition of 1909.]

From Chapter XXX 'Thorstein Goes Abroad'

When they came to Iceland they asked their way to Holyfell [1909: Helgafell], the homestead near the temple. It was easy to find, for every one knew the name and fame of it: and in a few days they came there, sailing Westward and Northward round the coast and in Breidafiord: but they learned that Thorstein Codbiter was dead, drowned in fishing a twelve-month ago come harvest-time. Thora was still there, keeping house for her child Thorgrim; and her brother Thord Gellir was a great man in the countryside. So the lads were in no lack of friends here as well as heretofore, and made hay while the sun shone.

Their goods were loaded on Thora's beasts, and brought up to her house. Thorstein Swart, who kept the temple, and stood as Godi until Thorgrim the child should grow old enough to take the priesthood of his father, he fixed the prices, according to custom; and then our lads were free to go about and trade with their neighbours. They sold their wares to such as wanted them; and those that would not have them at the price fixed, had them not at all.

There was much for a stranger to see in Iceland. At Thor's-ness [1909: Helgafell] there was the new temple, and its high-seats adorned with the old carved pillars that came from Norway, and that showed the way to Thorolf Mostbeard, when first he came off that coast and threw them overboard to drift ashore. And there was the inner house of the temple, rounded like the choir of a church, with the altar-stall, and the great ring lying upon it by which all oaths were sworn, and the blood-bowl and sprinkling-rod for the sacrifices, and the images of Thor and the gods standing round about. Outside there was the doom-ring with the stone of Thor, where men were sacrificed. [1909: And at the Thing-stead, on a low rocky point of land reaching out into the firth, with the islands of Breidafjord all around, and the snow-capped mountains of Bardastrand at the back of the water, there was the doom-ring; and a little way inland, beside the booths of the thing-men who came to the great meeting in summer, was the stone of Thor, where men were sacrificed.]

After they had done their business, the lads went with a party of their friends from Holyfell [1909: Helgafell], riding to the Iceland Althing; and they saw the wonderful valley with the precipices around and the deep rifts that seam it, and the throngs that come together year by year into the midst of that waste and terrible wilderness of frost and fire [1909: ...that come together year by year making a populous town of that waste and terrible wilderness].

But when they were safe returned and had taken leave of Thora, they made ready for their voyage to Norway: for they had a mind to see the old home of their kin, and to come before king Hakon the good, the fosterling of Athelstan of England. So in the summer, when the days were long and seas were fair, they sailed east, and came safely to Throndheim.

[Note 2: Collingwood's main source for this passage is the early chapters of *Eyrbyggja saga*, translated into English as *The Story of the Ere-Dwellers* by William Morris and Eiríkr Magnússon in 1892; in some places he follows it very closely. In making his main addition in 1909, Collingwood seems to have had his 1897 watercolour of Thor's Stone in front of him (see page 48).]

Matthew Townend

Appendix 8: The Collingwood Icelandic Pilgrimage, 18-25 July 2012

In July 2012, 33 'pilgrims' from the CWAAS spent a very memorable week in Iceland, visiting interesting historical sites, saga-steads and museums, while enjoying the dramatic landscape and the Icelandic food. The group was splendidly led and guided by Dr Matthew Townend, University of York and Dr Emily Lethbridge of the Árni Magnússon Institute for Icelandic Studies, Reykjavík. Among the pilgrims were members of the Collingwood family, including W.G. Collingwood's granddaughter, Teresa Smith. Everywhere we were treated with the most generous hospitality. A comprehensive account has been written by Graham Avery (2013).

Mike Lea/Aron

The Collingwood group at Borg Church:
Emily Lethbridge and Matthew Townend are seated at the front

Graham Avery

Matthew Townend comparing the view from Helgafell with W.G. Collingwood's drawing

Mike Lea

Emily Lethbridge reading *Njáls saga* at Hlíðarendi

A Symposium on W.G. Collingwood in Iceland

was held on the 19th July in the Þjóðminjasafn Íslands (the National Museum of Iceland), starting with an exhibition of some of his Icelandic paintings. Teresa Smith had recently found the original map of Iceland used and annotated by W.G.C. in 1897. She formally presented this to Lilja Árnadóttir, the Collections Manager of the National Museum, in recognition of his importance in Iceland. This was reported in the newspaper *Morgunblaðið* and on Icelandic TV.

Mike Lea

Presentation of the map used by W.G. Collingwood in 1897

Matthew Townend then talked about 'W.G. Collingwood and Iceland', focussing on Collingwood's interest and activity in the field of Norse culture before and after his visit to Iceland. He showed some drawings of Viking costumes by W.G.C. which have recently been found. He was followed by Einar Falur Ingólfsson, the Icelandic photographer and author of *Sögustaðir: Í fótspor W.G. Collingwoods* ('Saga-Steads: In the Footsteps of W.G. Collingwood'). He explained that 'Tourists with no knowledge of the region always ask for a guide': about pilgrims and photographs from travels. Einar has spent several years taking photographs of the sites of the Collingwood paintings and tracing the history of the places and people W.G.C. visited and met. He is a real enthusiast! We then enjoyed a Reception given by the English Speaking Union in Iceland. Many thanks to all who helped to arrange these events.

Alfresco Feasts in 1897 and 2012

1897: 'We first had to climb the steep crag onto the island, and then an **alfresco feast** awaited us. There we sat in the sunshine with a horn of plenty and looked down upon Stykkishólmur. There were many speeches and the words were big, as is customary with the Icelanders, when they finally loosen their tongue-tied nature in a crowd.' **Jón Stefánsson**

'. . . had a picnic on an island with a lot of people who sang songs and I sketched.' **W.G. Collingwood**

Graham Avery

Our Icelandic feast

2012: Rakel Olsen of Stykkishólmur had long wanted to recreate the 1897 alfresco feast on the island of Súgandisey (now part of the harbour) and we were delighted when she invited us to join her! A warm welcome at an open-air wine reception on the jetty (in the pouring rain, just like home) was followed by the most splendid Icelandic feast in the town, then by a talk by Matthew, stories by Ingi Hans Jónsson and songs by Sigurbjörg Kristin Hannesdóttir.

An unforgettable occasion!

Mike and Kate Lea

The Variance of *Njáls saga* - Gráskinna

W.G. Collingwood went to Iceland in the first place because of the Icelandic sagas and their relation to the landscape. The 2012 Pilgrimage visited Þjóðmenningarhúsið (the Culture House) in Reykjavík to look at some early saga manuscripts and to learn about research on them. They later visited many of the saga-sites, including from *Njáls saga*, which is is one of the most famous of the Íslendingasögu and is set in the south of Iceland.

Njáls saga is preserved in around 60 manuscripts, 21 of which are parchment manuscripts produced between 1300-1600. This is an unusually large number of early manuscripts but no single one contains the whole text of the saga. Six, however, contain the bulk of it: these are Reykjabók (AM 468 4to), c.1300-1325; Gráskinna (GKS 2870 4to, pictured), c.1300 with additions from c.1500-1550; Möðruvallabók (AM 132 fol.), c.1330-1370; Kálfalækjarbók (AM 133 fol.), c.1350; Skafinskinna (GKS 2868 4to), c.1350-1400; Oddabók (AM 466 4to), c.1460.

These early manuscripts testify to the saga's enduring popularity. The fact that no two manuscript texts are alike also demonstrates how those who copied the saga were free to alter the text as they saw fit. At the Stofnun Árna Magnússonar (Árni Magnússon Institute) in Reykjavík we now have a major research project entitled 'The Variance of *Njáls saga'*, to investigate aspects of the transmission of *Njáls saga*. Our aim is not to define a lost archetype or 'original author's version' but to understand the variations. The fragile Gráskinna ('Grey skin') manuscript is shown here.

Emily Lethbridge
Stofnun Árna Magnússonar

The Gráskinna manuscript of *Njáls saga*

Appendix 9: W.G. Collingwood in Iceland - a short bibliography

Avery, Graham (2013) *The Collingwood Icelandic Pilgrimage 2012,* Little Musgrave: CWAAS.

Collingwood, Jeremy (2012) *A Lakeland Saga. The Story of the Collingwood and Altounyan Family in Coniston and Aleppo,* Ammanford: Sigma Leisure.

Collingwood, W.G. (1895) *Thorstein of the Mere*. London: Edward Arnold (revised edition 1909 Kendal:Titus Wilson). Full text on http://www.allthingsransome.net/literary/thorhtm2.htm

Collingwood, W.G. (1896)*The Bondwoman*. London: Edward Arnold.

Collingwood, W.G. and Stefánsson, Jón (1899) *A Pilgrimage to the Saga-steads of Iceland* Ulverston: Holmes. Facsimile from British Library, Historical Print Editions.

Collingwood, W.G. and Stefánsson, Jón (1902) *The Life and Death of Cormac the Skald.* (Viking Club Translation Series No.1). Ulverston: Holmes.
Full text online at sagadb.org/kormaks_saga.en

Gnosspelius Janet (1996) *Letters from Iceland, Collingwood Studies* Vol. Three, pp. ix-xi, 1-75, Swansea: R.G. Collingwood Society.

Hannesson, Haraldur (1969) *W.G. Collingwood Á söguslóðum*, Reykjavík: Bókaútgáfa Menningarsjóðs.

Hannesson, H., Björnsson, Á. S., Björnsson, B. Th., and Gnosspelius, J.B. (1988) *Fegurð Íslands og fornir sögustaðir*, Reykjavík: Bókaútgáfan Örn og Örlygur hf.

Ingólfsson, Einar Falur (2010) *Sögustaðir - Í fótspor W.G. Collingwoods* ('Saga-steads - In the footsteps of W.G. Collingwood'), Reykjavík: Crymogea.

Morris, William (1871 and 1873) *Icelandic Journals*, Gary L. Aho (ed.), online edition, morrisedition.lib.uiowa.edu/icelandicdiaries.html

Overing, Gillian R. and Osborn, Marijane (1994) *Landscape of Desire,* Minneapolis: University of Minnesota Press.

Stefánsson, Jón (1949) *Úti í Heimi*, Reykjavík: Bókellsútgáfan h.f.

Townend, Matthew (2009) *The Vikings and Victorian Lakeland: The Norse Medievalism of W.G. Collingwood and his Contemporaries*, Kendal: CWAAS Extra Series XXXIV.

Wawn, Andrew (2000) *The Vikings and the Victorians,* Cambridge: D.S. Brewer.

Web-sites, YouTube and Podcasts

'Collingwood, W.G.', en.wikipedia.org/wiki/W._G._Collingwood

'MYNDIR W. G. COLLINGWOODS (Coll.)', Collingwood's paintings in Þjóðminjasafn Íslands, ljosmyndasafnislands.is/ljosmyndir/gallery.asp?categoryid=197

'Icelandic Saga Database', sagadb.org

Lethbridge, Emily, 'The Saga-Steads of Iceland - A 21st-century Pilgrimage', sagasteads.blogspot.com/
'Cambridge Ideas - Memories of Old Awake': www.youtube.com/watch?v=2Z4_BhW1sl8
BBC History Magazine: Podcast 17 May 2012.

'The Saga-Steads of Collingwood & Einar Falur Ingólfsson', www.youtube.com/watch?v=5jsRqUibUVE

'Travels in 19th-century Iceland', northernlite.ca/19thcenturyiceland/

'Southward bound . .'

'And, southward bound, after these months of eager sight-seeing, we can at last reckon up what we have viewed, and what we have missed; asking ourselves—Was it worth while, our pilgrimage to the Saga-steads?

We have missed, we must confess, nearly all that attracts the tourists. Iceland is not to be judged from our pages. We have not explored the crater of Hekla, nor the sulphur-mines of Krísuvík: we took only a distant peep of the Geysir and the basalt freaks of Stapi; into Surt's Cave we just glanced, and crossed in silence the vast rivers and waste reaches of the inland wilderness. None of the greatest waterfalls, or glaciers, or volcanoes come into our tale,—nothing of the marvels of frost and fire that so many have been anxious to see, and so few have really penetrated and described.

Nor, again, have we gossiped as we might of the peasantry and their quaint, old-world life, so charming and picturesque, interesting alike to the antiquary and the artist. There is quite a new world for the painter in Iceland,—in sensational landscape and in pastoral subjects; but all this was not in our programme.

Our one desire was to find the scenes of long ago,—to put a background to the figures of history: and this we have done. Though there are a few minor sagas left without illustration, we may claim to have carried out our enterprise. We have seen the homes of the heroes. They are no longer empty names to us, no longer formless dreams; and with their reality the great dramas of old start into life and action. It is as if a curtain had gone suddenly up: as if our eyes were opened, at last, to the glory of the North.'

W.G. Collingwood and Jón Stefánsson
A Pilgrimage to the Saga-steads of Iceland